CW01468340

THE COMPLETE

TRIP IN A VAN
GUIDE TO AUSTRALIA

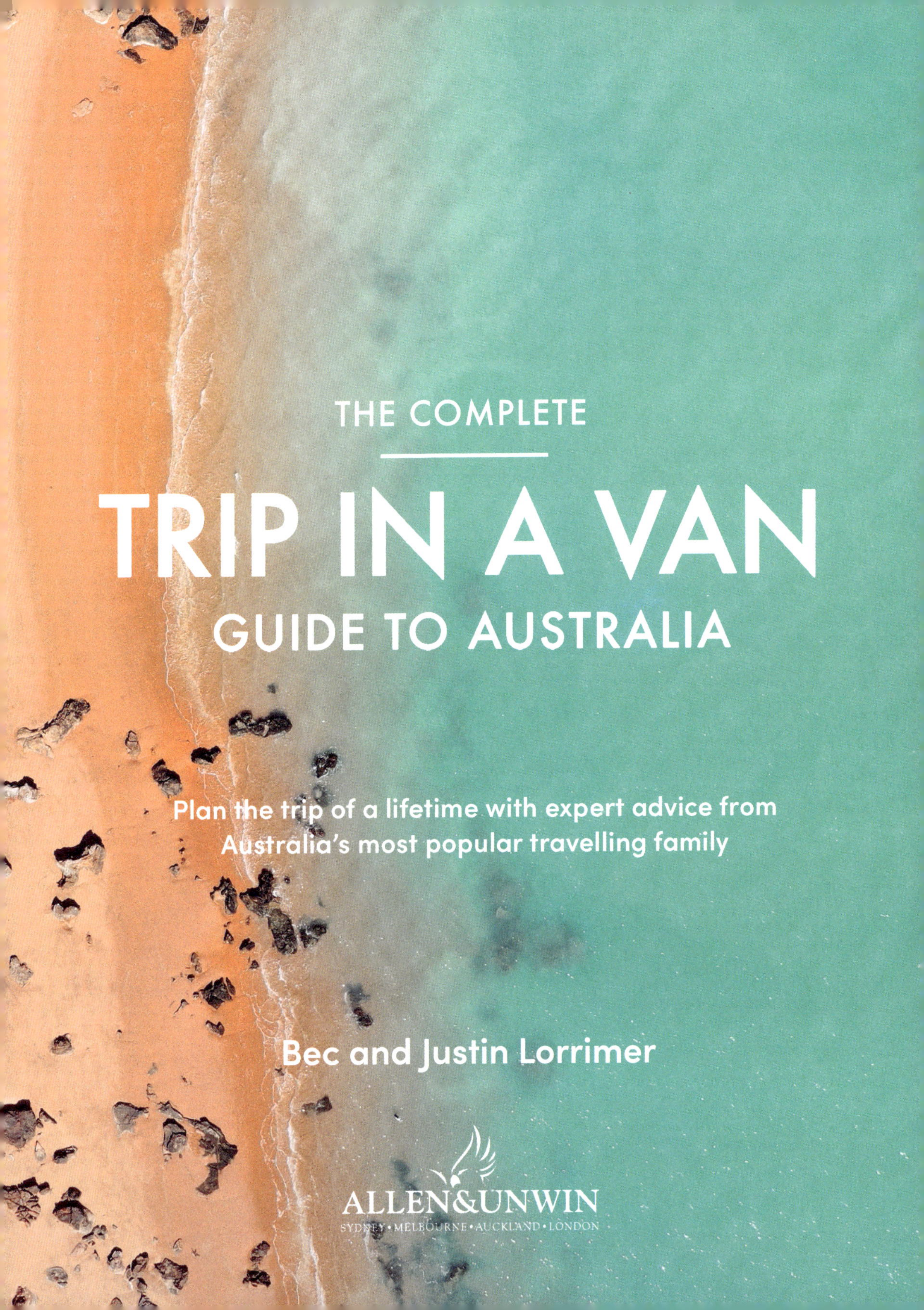

THE COMPLETE

TRIP IN A VAN

GUIDE TO AUSTRALIA

Plan the trip of a lifetime with expert advice from
Australia's most popular travelling family

Bec and Justin Lorrimer

ALLEN&UNWIN
SYDNEY · MELBOURNE · AUCKLAND · LONDON

Contents

Hello 7

Hello!

We're Bec and Justin, and in 2015 we decided to take our three young kids away on a trip of a lifetime. We had just had our third baby, and Justin was doing shift work in the mines. His mental health had started to decline and the constraints of work were consuming him. There was little time for family, and something needed to change. We bought a caravan and embarked on what we thought would be a twelve-month trip around Australia. Seven years later, we're still travelling indefinitely.

Our children Jack, Billy and Charli thrive on the lifestyle, experiences and quality time with us. They are the most well-rounded, resilient, carefree and happy kids. You really can't put a price on time with your children.

The simplicity of the travel lifestyle, the family bonding time and the landscapes of Australia are what we love most about caravanning. We are passionate about making a conscious decision to unplug from the daily grind and connect with each other. Making memories and exploring Australia was fulfilling a lifelong dream, and now it's a lifestyle and career as we share our knowledge and experiences from our time on the road.

This book will guide you through the period leading up to your departure and your time on the road—it's got everything we wish we'd known before we started! This complete guide is the culmination of seven years travelling Australia full-time, and whether you're dreaming about a trip, prepping your caravan to start or already on the road, we're stoked to have you with us.

Let's get into it!

PART 1

—

Before You Go

Planning

Set a date

The very first thing you need to do when you're planning a trip is set a date and stick to it. I can't stress this enough. If you set a goal to work towards, it really is amazing what you can achieve. We set off just ten weeks after committing to the decision, and that included selling our house and belongings before hitting the road. That's not necessarily a timeline I would advise, as it was pretty hectic to say the least. But it did light a fire in our bellies and our excitement really threw us into gear!

If you don't set a date, that party you've got coming up, the wedding invitation on your fridge or your nephew's birthday will keep you at home. Set a date and tell everyone you're committed to leaving on that date. Not only will it prepare you socially, it will also give you a financial goal and some motivation to hit the road.

Packing up your home

You're about to set off on your travels and with mixed emotions you're trying to pack up your home! Congratulations on taking one of the biggest leaps and deciding to travel Australia.

Packing it all in for the adventure of a lifetime is daunting! We think it's a courageous decision but it's also one you'll be forever grateful you made.

Your weekends will be officially over leading up to departure because you will be packing up your house, cleaning, making countless trips to the rubbish tip and answering the door to strangers from Gumtree who are buying your possessions. But this preparation is all part of the excitement. Deciding what to take on your travels, de-cluttering and getting rid of the things you don't need is a stressful and liberating experience. The fact of the matter

is that you are about to live a simple life and you really don't need many possessions.

Start by selling off furniture that you know you can go without until you leave. Things you might have in a second living area or the toy room. Do you have a second car you need to put up for sale? Cardboard boxes are your best friend when you're packing up your home. We needed a *lot*, so to avoid buying them, we posted ads on community Facebook groups and Facebook Marketplace, as well as the BuySwapSell groups. You will usually snap up some free boxes. Saving money on cardboard boxes might seem like small change but trust us: it all helps when you're planning the trip of a lifetime.

Storage

Some belongings and sentimental items can't easily be thrown out, sold or taken with you on your travels, so you'll need to find a place to store them. If you have family or friends who can offer you storage space on their property, you will be saving a huge amount in storage fees. However, if that's not an option, there are still plenty of options.

Storing your 'stuff' with a professional storage company is a great option—get a quote for a storage company in your area to compare prices. Choose an annual plan and pay upfront: this ensures that you won't have any direct debits on your travels and is often cheaper.

To give you an idea of cost, we have a 3 metre x 1.3 metre storage shed and pay an annual cost of $1200. Another option is to buy a storage container and leave it on a family member's or friend's property.

Storage containers can be picked up online before you go and then sold on your return. Take a look on Gumtree or Facebook Marketplace for one in your area.

Mail

When you do head off on your travels, you'll need to consider mail. How do you receive it? Bills, schoolwork, written correspondence?

Firstly, convert all the paper mail you usually receive to online delivery so you'll instead receive it via your email. Typically there is an option to do this online, but you may need to allocate a few hours to making phone calls too.

Next, download the Australia Post app. This is excellent for tracking your deliveries and also for adding your addresses along the way while you travel. Create a login, add your details and locate a post office or parcel locker in the area you'd like to have your items sent. It's online shopping made easy while you travel. It's also super easy to receive schoolwork if your kids are doing remote learning.

Parcel lockers are fantastic as they allow you to have your parcel sent to a locker (usually in a CBD) meaning you won't have to enter the post office. You will receive a notification via SMS that your parcel has arrived and it's kept in the locker for 48 hours. If you are unable to pick it up in this time, it is sent to the post office for you to pick up there. Australia Post will hold your parcel for ten days before returning it to the sender.

A week before you leave home, organise a mail redirection, which will ensure you haven't missed any mail you'd meant to make paperless or redirect. This is especially important if you have sold up. Finally, if you require paper mail to be sent to you, for example information on rates or water, have it redirected to a family member's or friend's address. A redirection for three months is advised. If you're like us and have forgotten a few redirections (for mail such as super), it is as easy as a family member opening our mail and us making a quick call to have it changed.

Which direction to travel? Anti-clockwise or clockwise?

Which direction and what time of the year should you travel Australia? This hugely depends on when you want to leave and where you're starting your trip.

In our experience, to maintain a fair-weather lifestyle and miss cyclone season and the humidity, you need to stick with the seasons. That means travelling down south to Tassie and across the bottom of Australia's coastline in the summer months and aiming to be in the north from Broome across to the top end of Cairns between the months of May and September. It starts to get very hot and humid when September rolls around and the 'build up' begins morphing into the wet season.

There are plenty of theories about how going clockwise is ideal for fuel economy because of the winds, but having now driven the lap of Australia in both directions, we didn't notice a change in fuel consumption.

Even if there was a difference, it would only be a few hundred dollars and not enough to warrant changing your direction of travel.

For us, departing from NSW or Victoria in January is ideal, and we prefer to travel clockwise. Many travellers typically travel this way, so the chances of meeting like-minded people and families are higher. It is also a great way to catch up again at different points along the way.

Leaving NSW or Victoria in January means you are in South Australia throughout February and down in the southwest corner in March, allowing you to make your way up the west coast to be in Broome by about June.

Spend three months across the top and down the centre and then aim to be in Cape York and Cairns in September. This enables you to spend the rest of the year travelling down the east coast, staying warm throughout, and to be home for Christmas in NSW or Victoria.

Caravanning is an outdoor lifestyle, so you really don't want to be too cold or in the midst of a cyclone.

Money

Making a travel budget is an important part of preparing for your trip around Australia.

How much you're able to save and budget plays a huge part in how long you can travel for. Planning ahead and preparing for everything is the key to avoiding any spending shocks.

We calculated our expenses based on the trip we were planning, taking into consideration the number of kilometres we were going to travel, how much free camping we intended on doing and the cost of feeding our family of five. It's also always worth considering big ticket activities such as a whale shark swim in Exmouth, WA, or a Horizontal Falls flight in the Kimberley. Do your research and budget for as much as you can before you leave—it'll save you lots of stress down the line.

Fuel

The most basic way to estimate your fuel costs is by deciding on a timeframe for your trip and approximately how many kilometres you'll be travelling, then calculating your fuel expenses based on the current petrol price. We use an excellent app called 'Fuel Map' which keeps a record of money spent on fuel as well as L/100km. It will also calculate your average cost per fill. It usually costs $12,000–15,000 in fuel to do a full lap of Australia. But with petrol prices increasingly rising over the last few years, it's definitely worth keeping a buffer in your budget for extra fuel costs.

Food

A weekly food bill is easily determined by your current grocery bill, although you do need to account for prices in remote areas, as groceries tend to be more expensive—sometimes up to twenty per cent more—the further you are from major centres. We are a family of five and budget for approximately $450–500 a week. In remote areas we expect to pay anywhere from $50 to $100 extra per week.

Accommodation

Deciding on how much you will free camp and how often you will stay in a caravan park will also help you figure out your weekly budget. We have varied our accommodation preferences over the years.

Our first two years were about 60 per cent caravan parks and 40 per cent free or low-cost camps. The price of caravan parks has really inflated since we began our travels in 2015, so now we stay at low-cost/free camps or farm stays around 80 per cent of the time because we simply cannot afford to blow out our budget. Caravan parks are now on average $55 a night for a powered site—and often there are extra charges of anywhere between $5 and $15 per child. That being said, the facilities at caravan parks can be a welcome change, and may suit your style of travel better than free camps.

Budgeting

The most important part of travelling Australia is ensuring you have the money to do so.

As a guide to help work out what you will spend while travelling, take a look at the sample budget spreadsheet on pages 278-81 or scan the QR code there to purchase and download a copy of the spreadsheet calculator from our website.

It covers all expenses from food, fuel and accommodation to insurances, phone bills and unexpected costs. For our family of five, we work off a rough expenditure of $1500 per week.

Therefore, if you're travelling for twelve months, you're looking at an estimated yearly expenditure of $78,000 on top of the purchase of your 4WD and caravan/

motorhome/camper trailer. Of course, you can definitely do it cheaper by mostly free camping, budgeting on food and so on—but don't let it compromise your holiday. This is a trip you'll never forget, and you want to experience as much as you can and be as comfortable as possible.

Now, we're in no position to give out financial advice but all we can say is: start saving!

If you need to push back your departure date and save a little longer to have yourself set up properly, then do it. We have met travellers who wished they had just saved a little longer and made their set-up more comfortable and functional for their trip. Once you set a date, begin by refining your expenses and selling the things you don't need, such as tools, baby items and furniture.

We set up a travel account and had a direct debit of $100 going into it every week on payday. We sold our camper trailer and were frugal with where we spent our money.

We stopped eating out, rarely bought coffee and never had takeaway.

Go through your bank statement and figure out where you can make savings—it's incredible how the little things add up. If you're struggling to adjust your spending or figure out where to start, consider seeking some professional advice to get you on the right track for your goals.

If you own your own home, consider whether renting it out will provide you with enough of a passive income to get by, or alternatively, think about using some of the profits from the sale of your home to help fund your travels. Another option is to take your job on the road. Can you work remotely? Or have an online business. Talk to your boss about working while you travel—in the post-pandemic world it's more common than you think.

Money saving tips

Save before you go

- Sell all the belongings that you do not need.
- Cancel your house cleaner.
- Cancel subscriptions and any unnecessary direct debits.
- Buy pre-loved clothes and goods. Scope out op shops.
- Don't eat out, opt to cook at home and take a packed lunch to work.
- Downsize your house and pocket the change.
- Service your own vehicle.
- Write a shopping list and stick to it. Don't be fooled into buying specials.
- Price check online quotes. Make sure you are getting the best price on insurances.
- Try home beauty. Tint and pluck your own eyebrows, paint your own nails, cut your kids' hair and dye your own hair.

Save on accommodation

- Sign up to loyalty clubs (e.g. G'Day Rewards) with caravan park chains—they are definitely worth it and you generally make your money back on your first booking.
- Book online where you can, as most parks have online discounts or 'Pay 3, Stay 4' deals.
- Travel Saver cards through your insurance company can save you a lot of money. We are insured with CIL and they provide lots of discounts on parks and attractions.
- Visit tourist information centres—grab some brochures for the local area you're in. They provide discount coupons for tours and attractions as well as restaurants.
- Free camp where you can, but don't compromise the enjoyment of your trip just to save a few bucks. Caravan parks have some prime real estate around the country and don't forget how long it might have taken you to drive to the other side of the country. It'll cost you a lot more than a night's accommodation to get back there if you skip it because you're being stingy!

- Invest in a TAWK (Travelling Australia With Kids) membership for a one-off fee of $40. This gets you two 'kids stay free' nights at a huge list of parks and stations around the country.

Save on food

- If you have the room, buy in bulk, cook in bulk and freeze meals. It's cheaper and easier than stocking up on the run. We utilise the fridge in our canopy to buy large slabs of meat and store meals.
- Buy meat in bulk from local butchers on your way around—it can save you more than if you were to purchase pieces in a big chain supermarket. A whole rump can be as little as $12/kg if you buy it whole, whereas if you purchase just a few pieces in Woolies it's around $25/kg. Get the butcher to cut it up for you and freeze it in meal size portions.
- Stock up at the big chain supermarkets and plan your major grocery shops in bigger town centres before you head to remote areas or the outback, as this can save you hundreds of dollars.

Save on fuel

- Keep your weight down and travel as light as you can. Do not travel with full water tanks unless you're going off grid (1 litre of water = 1kg) or your caravan manufacturer recommends travelling with full water tanks for stability.
- Get your tyre pressure right—less rolling resistance means better fuel economy.
- Find an economical cruising speed—use your vehicle's computer information to find out what speed is best for your fuel consumption and stick to it.
- Buy quality fuel as it will give you better fuel economy—we always use BP and recommend it to everyone.
- Utilise loyalty cards and shopping docket savings. It all helps!

Buying a van

Choosing your set-up

Deciding on your set-up is a really big decision. Car and caravan? Bus? Camper trailer? Van or motorhome?

The first thing to consider is what kind of travel you want to do. Remote trips that hit those dirt roads or adventures that keep your wheels on the bitumen? Do you want to stick to coastal towns or go off-grid in more regional areas? Would you prefer caravan parks or free camps? These are all questions that it is important to ask yourself before purchasing the perfect set-up.

We considered all of those factors and decided to buy a caravan. We decided we wanted to travel on dirt roads, go off-grid, discover coastal beach camps and do some caravan parks as well. All these preferences brought us to our ultimate set-up of a chopped 200 series LandCruiser and a Sunseeker Desert Storm. Keep in mind, you do not need this set-up to travel Australia. If you want to travel like we have, what we would advise is getting a capable caravan that will suit your needs.

There really is so much to choose from in the caravanning market, so go and look at them all and get a feel for the layout and quality you are happy to pay for.

Things to consider when buying a caravan

Interior

- To live on the road you'll require a toilet and shower. It really is essential in making your trip enjoyable. An added consideration is that many beach camps and campgrounds actually require you to be self-contained in order to camp there.
- Having to push out beds or lift a pop-top gets old quickly. In a pop-top your belongings may not be as safe as in a van and you'll really feel those cold nights, because pop-tops have poor insulation.
- Sturdy suspension and the type of suspension—such as dirt-road-capable, air bag, on-road or off-road suspension—will determine where you can take your caravan and should be well thought out.
- An island bed is essential in our opinion, and far superior to an east–west bed (which doesn't allow easy access on both sides). It wouldn't be fun climbing over each other to get in and out of bed, let alone at 2am when nature calls.
- Big windows mean lots of light and a breeze on those warm days.
- Get a washing machine. Full stop. Even better if it is installed into your caravan. You'll save money and you won't have to line up to wait for a machine in a caravan park or laundromat.
- Make sure your bunks are roomy enough for your kids. Get them to jump in, roll around and sit up in them. You may need to consider extending them or taking away under bed storage for more space as this is their 'bedroom' and an area for themselves. Our kids play Lego and watch movies in their beds and this is their downtime away from each other.
- Storage! Wherever you can build in storage, do it. Everything needs a place. Everything! We had a footrest on our lounge as standard, but we had it removed and made the space into a drawer. This now houses all our shoes.
- Bench space. You need a lot of it, so if you can extend your kitchen without compromising your payload and weight, do it.
- Forget hanging space in your cupboards! You will lose loads of room to store things you wear daily such as shorts and singlets.
- Do you need an oven? It really is a personal decision. We have had one before and found that we mostly used it for food storage. We cook a lot on our Weber and use it as an oven rather than give up space in our kitchen.
- Magazine pockets are a great way to store schoolwork, iPads and tourism brochures while you travel.
- USB ports inside the kids' beds are handy if they are watching a movie or charging their iPads.
- Fans. We recommend Sirocco fans—they are by far the best. They're quiet and draw little current, saving your battery. Have one installed in each bunk and two over the main bed, so that one of them can be turned around to your kitchen/dining area.
- A decent caravan mattress is a must. Don't try and make a saving here, especially if you will be sleeping on it long-term. Opt for a pillow top. We have a top of the range caravan mattress which came with our caravan and we rate it highly!

Exterior

- A rear bar on the caravan enables you to mount things like spare tyres, generator boxes, jerry can holders and bike racks. You can also mount a folding boat trailer like we have.
- A stone guard is a great addition to protect the front of your van from stone chips on all those outback roads.
- Having a longer drawbar allows you to fit a storage box on the front, which provides great storage outside your caravan.

Tare, ATM, payload and tow ball weights explained

Tare
The tare weight of a caravan is its base weight as it leaves the factory floor.

ATM (Aggregate Trailer Mass)
The ATM is the total weight your caravan can legally weigh with all your gear in it.

Payload
The payload of your caravan is your ATM minus your TARE weight.

Tow ball weight
Tow ball weight is the amount in kilograms that your caravan hitch puts onto the tow ball of your car.

**ATM
3500kg**

**Tare weight
2650kg**

**3500kg—2650kg
= 850kg**

**Payload
850kg**

Tip

If you're travelling full time, you will need as much payload as you can in your caravan. Once you have packed in all your gear and filled up all your water tanks you will be searching for more payload.

Solar and batteries

Another investment we would recommend—though it's not a necessity—is an excellent battery system. How much free camping you will do and for how long will determine what kind of battery system you will require.

We have a 400amp/h off-grid system with 720 watts of solar that powers our whole van as if plugged into a powered site.

Our washing machine, coffee machine, blender, camera and computer chargers, hair straightener and air conditioner all run off the inverter and battery system.

If you're planning to do a lot of free camping, a battery system like ours will pay for itself as you'll save big on expensive site fees at caravan parks.

Suspension

If you can protect your van from shaking and rattling over rough roads, you'll have fewer breakages and your van will last longer. The only way to do this is to fit quality suspension that suits your travels.

We have had over four years of trouble-free touring and have always used Cruisemaster suspension.

These guys are the leader in quality caravan suspension in Australia. We are currently using the Cruisemaster ATX full air suspension on our Desert Storm.

Grey water tanks

A grey water tank catches all your shower and kitchen sink drain water, so that you can dispose of it elsewhere. Lots of campgrounds are now stipulating that campers must have a grey water tank fitted in order to stay.

Water tanks

Tanks are always fitted as standard on a caravan, but you can always add more. Our recommendation is to fit as many tanks as your ATM will allow.

Having fresh water for drinking, showers and dishes definitely makes life easier while you're off-grid.

Awnings and annexes

There are a range of different awnings to choose from, but our tip is to purchase a quality brand like Dometic. We have had years of trouble-free use from ours. Cheaper alternatives tend to be weaker in windy conditions.

Unless you plan to stop for long periods of time in cold conditions, don't bother taking an annexe with you. They are bulky, heavy and take up valuable storage space.

The car

Vehicle winch

There is a lot of choice in the winch market, especially with all the cheap imported options around these days. But if you want a reliable winch that you can use time and time again on your travels around Australia, it's worth looking into more reputable brands.

We have used two different winches on our travels and both have been great. On our Mazda BT50 we had a Warn winch. On our LandCruiser we have fitted a Bushranger 4x4 Revo 12S.

The great thing about having a winch is that you have the ability to recover yourself when you get bogged in off-road situations, rather than waiting for help. We have even used it to pull our caravan in and out of tight camp spots.

Suspension

All vehicles that will be touring and towing big loads will need some sort of suspension upgrade. We recommend you consult the experts about your particular vehicle to discuss your requirements. Your first stop should be your local ARB 4x4 dealer to have a chat about your needs.

From our experience over the years, the perfect set-up for towing a caravan around the country is a 2-inch lift with upgraded springs to suit your towing weights. Remember, as the saying goes, 'You get what you pay for.'

A bull bar

For us a bull bar is essential but for a lot of other travellers it is not. We think they offer great frontal protection for your vehicle and also enable a winch to be fitted, but do your research and decide for yourself!

UHFs

A UHF is an essential part of road tripping around Australia. Maintaining communication with other roads users is integral to a safe and well-informed trip. You can use a UHF to stay in contact with other travellers when you're in convoy and also to communicate with trucks when you need to overtake. It also allows other travellers to inform you of hazards ahead, such as accidents or road works.

We have always used Oricom UHF radios and recommend them as an affordable and good quality solution. We use the DTX4200 Ultimate Touring Pack and country antenna.

Wheels and tyres

Look for quality alloy wheels that are load rated for your vehicle's GVM (Gross Vehicle Mass) and a good quality all-terrain tyre. You don't want to buy cheap wheels and tyres because they will only let you down. Stick with reputable companies.

Roof racks

This decision will depend on whether you need extra storage up on top, which most full-time travellers do. We use the ARB Base Rack to store our swags, recovery tracks and shovel full-time. It's a great place to put items you don't use very often to keep them out of the way.

Dual battery system

Having a second battery and charger in your tow vehicle is a must for long-term travel. The ability to run a second fridge/freezer is not only convenient on day trips, but also allows you to store more food when you are remote camping away from towns and grocery stores. A good system can be expensive and requires careful instalment to operate correctly, so if you're unsure, contact your local auto electrician for some guidance.

Our advice would be to look at a quality 120 amp hour (AH) AGM battery and a 40 amp DC/DC charger. If your budget allows, you should look into lithium to save some weight.

Vehicle storage

Your storage options will depend on the type of vehicle you have. The ultimate in touring storage is a dedicated unit fitted to your vehicle, like our Norweld canopy, but there are lots of other options for those travelling in wagons and dual cabs. The most common storage additions are a good set of storage draws and containers. These give all your gear a home and make it easy to organise and access.

Roadside assistance

Roadside assistance is extremely important when you're travelling Australia, especially when you're travelling to remote places.

We can tell you this from experience: we broke down in between Katherine and Darwin in the Northern Territory. We had blown a

hose and the car overheated, so given it was an extremely hot day, we were glad we had assistance within the hour.

Our advice is to get full cover for complete peace of mind for you and your family. We have roadside cover with RACV—our policy is called Total Care. It costs us around $250 for the year. When we had our breakdown situation, we were towed to the nearest town, put up in accommodation, provided with a hire car and flown to a town of our choice, which was Cairns. All covered and not an extra cent paid.

So when purchasing your roadside assistance, suss out the benefits of each policy and ensure you are covered for a generous number of towing kilometres.

Insurance

Once again, insurance for your vehicle and caravan is really an individual decision. Our caravan is insured through CIL, which has contents included. Our LandCruiser is insured through Club 4x4. We chose this company because they provide the best cover for off-roading and remote touring, which suits our needs.

What to pack

The packing list

Where do you even start when you're packing for months and months on the road? It is very hard to know what you will need to travel Australia, especially if you have never done it before.

Our best piece of advice would be to take a short trip in your set-up before heading off on your maiden voyage. If that's not an option, sleep in the backyard and get a feel for what you'll need.

We have a lot more now than when we started! But we began with the bare minimum and purchased more 'things' along the way, especially as our kids grew. Your payload won't allow you to bring everything and you won't have the storage or space to travel with everything you owned in your static house. As a rule of thumb, less is more.

To give you a basic foundation for what you'll need to pack, see our useful checklist on pages 282–87.

Bikes, scooters and surfboards

This is a tough one and a very individual decision. Keep in mind that from Exmouth in WA across the Top End to Agnes Water in Queensland, it's not possible to surf. So if you're planning to travel mostly in the Top End, I would avoid taking surfboards—if you have a desire to surf you can always hire a board.

Bikes have always gotten really good use from our kids, but we have met families whose kids don't miss them at all. Our advice is to avoid taking expensive bikes with you, as caravan parks can have thieves and the bikes will get heavily damaged living on the outside of your car/caravan, or rusty from being open to the elements all the time. Our kids love riding their scooters, but they can only ride them when there is bitumen around, which isn't always the case when free camping or in national parks.

Toys

Before we left home, I gave Jack and Billy a backpack and told them to fill it with their favourite toys as these would be the only ones we would take on our trip. For baby Charli, I packed a couple of hanging plush toys for the car, a rattle and a few other toys. Since then, we have purchased extra toys and Lego, but to be honest, kids really don't need much at all. We have one small tub for Lego/toys and they each have their favourites at the end of their bed.

On the road, your kids will be too busy to play with toys. Your days will be filled with endless adventure—climbing trees, making new mates, riding bikes and swimming.

That being said, they need their down days too, so it's great to have a small tub of toys available.

Camera gear

How do you document a lap of Australia? Our big tip is to keep it simple. We recommend two camera essentials.

GoPro

If you can get your hands on a HERO10, they are brilliant and just as good as the HERO8. The HERO10 has a few more features, such as a media hub. If you want to document your travels and film underwater then a GoPro is pretty unbeatable. Plus, they're almost unbreakable and therefore great if you have kids. You can take still shots or video—it's a great all-round camera.

DSLR or mirrorless camera

Trust us when we say you'll see many picture-perfect sights on your trip that you will want to capture and put on your wall at home. In order to do this, you'll need a high-resolution camera. An iPhone could do the job in theory, but we recommend investing in something a little higher quality for capturing those really special moments.

Good floor matting

This is one item you don't want to skimp on! Having a quality floor mat might cost you a bit, but they are worth their weight in gold. They allow all the sand and dirt to fall through the mat outside your van before it makes its way inside. We recommend C-Gear annex flooring and also use a Muk Mat as a doormat.

A few 240 volt leads to reach every power box and a 10–15 amp adaptor

Not every powered site you pull up to will be the same. Sometimes the power box might be a long way from your van, which can be quite a drama if your leads aren't long enough. So you can either carry one really long lead (they can be super annoying to roll up), or you can carry two leads and only pull out the extra one when it's needed. We also carry an Amphibian power adaptor that allows us to plug into a 10 amp power source at a friend's or relative's place.

A few water hoses and a waste hose for the van, as well as a flexible one for an outdoor shower

It can be very annoying if you can't plug mains water into your van, so make sure you've got enough length in your hoses. And a good waste/sullage hose will run all your shower and kitchen sink water away from your campsite.

A range of different hose fittings, and hose bags to store the above

If you're like us, you will probably leave a few hose fittings attached to different taps around the country and not realise until you pull up at your next site and go to plug your hose in. We carry a Ziplock bag full of different hose fittings and joiners to cover any hose dramas we come across along the way.

A filter housing for dirty/bore water

Depending on where your travels take you, there is a good chance that you will come across bore water. We use an inline filter housing to filter our water either before we fill our tanks or before it plugs into our water mains on the van. The filter takes a lot of sediment and smell out of the water—you can also get filters that help remove bacteria.

Levelling ramps for those awkward sites

These little beauties are like gold! Nobody likes sleeping on a random tilt and constantly rolling towards your missus or the edge of the bed. An extra minute of set-up time to throw a levelling ramp under your caravan wheels can make a whole lot of difference to your comfort. We now have air suspension, so it is as simple as a push of a button to level ourselves up.

A battery impact gun or drill for the stabiliser legs

Some may say this isn't essential, and they may be right. But let me tell you, if you travel full-time, you will want one! We use ours to extend and retract our stabiliser legs when we set up. Yes, you can wind them up and down by hand, but trust me, it gets old fast. We carry an impact gun, but you can also use a cordless drill with a socket.

A range of different pegs and a good whacker

Short pegs, long pegs and Hex Pegs. You need a few different choices for the different types of ground you'll come across around the country. We invested in some Hex Pegs for securing our awning into tough ground; they are installed using the impact gun or drill and are perfect for securing your awning on windy days.

A trailer coupling lock to prevent/deter any would-be thieves

If someone really wants to steal your van, they probably will. But at least if you have a hitch lock fitted it will be a good deterrent for those would-be thieves looking for an easy target. There are some flash models around, and you generally get what you pay for. We now have a Cruisemaster off-road hitch on our van and it runs a cool bi-lock pin for security.

A whole heap of patience with your other half

Set-up and pack-up can be stressful at times, so be patient with each other. Who cares if it takes a few minutes longer—it just means the beer will be colder when you're ready!

PART 2

—

On the Road

Your first month on the road

It's important to remember you're undertaking a huge life change when you start your trip. When we started, we had three kids who had just been taken out of their home and put into a confined space called a caravan. Justin and I were suddenly in each other's pockets 24/7, plus he was now a stay-at-home dad and had to deal with the daytime tantrums, nappies and sleep schedules—that in itself is an adjustment! Some families slot into the travelling lifestyle easily, but it really did take a month or more for us to settle into life on the road.

The hardest part was settling the kids for sleep at night. We tried our best to keep them on their 7pm routine, but it was a really tough process as they were now sleeping on top of one another and could hear each other's cries and movements.

To add more complications into the mix, our six-month-old was teething and our two-year-old was having some dreaded night terrors. Justin and I also took a while to adjust to being together all day every day, which really isn't normal in modern family life. We argued and disagreed on almost everything, all while trying to remind ourselves to stay positive, patient and persistent.

Seven years on, we truly love the travelling lifestyle and our kids know it as the norm. It's hard to believe that we thought about turning back after that first month!

Travel basics

Booking accommodation

Our advice is don't book too far in advance. In all honesty, usually we don't book at all and just rock up to a caravan park or campsite. This enables you to change your plans, allow for weather conditions and travel with new friends. However, it's always worth booking in advance for school holidays—you can often do so online. We try to head inland to a bush camp, or park up with family or friends for those few weeks. It is always hectic along the coast as many families choose parks and campsites for their two weeks of school holidays, so do try to pre-empt this and sort your accommodation early.

Similarly, sought-after campsites such as Cape Range National Park always need booking in advance or you will not get a site.

When booking accommodation, it's worth asking if they have any special offers. Many station stays and caravan parks will offer a stay/pay deal such as 'stay 4, pay 3' or special prices for booking online.

Water saving and finding water

It's very easy to locate water while you're travelling, provided it is available. The WikiCamps app notes water points on the map. This will give you directions to the nearest water tap where you can fill up your tanks, but be sure to check if it is drinking water, non-potable water or treated water.

Water saving tips

1. Carry baby wipes with you—they are always handy when you're cleaning up or giving yourself a bird bath.
2. Only do your dishes once a day.
3. Switch your washing machine to a quick load (if your battery system allows this), as this will save on litres used. Alternatively, look into carrying a Scrubba Wash Bag or do it the old-school way and handwash your clothes in a bucket with detergent, then rinse and hang out.
4. For many campers, showering out on the tracks is a luxury, especially when travelling remotely. A small amount of water and a flannel can do the job just fine. Limit your showering to save on water and bathe the kids in a tub!

Wifi/internet

If you plan on taking work on the road with you, then Wifi or an internet connection are essential. There are many options out there, but we recommend choosing Telstra as your provider. They have by far the best coverage around Australia, including in Indigenous communities, on stations and in remote areas.

We use the hotspot function on our phones and connect our TV, laptops and iPads—you just have to make sure you have plenty of mobile data. However, you can also purchase a separate modem or Wifi unit and pay monthly for this service. It all depends on how much data you have and how often you use it. Having a mobile signal booster is handy in areas that give you low coverage. Investigate companies such as Cel-Fi Go or Out There Internet.

Streaming

We find free-to-air TV can get pretty mundane, so we like to use streaming apps such as Netflix and Stan. We do this through a Chromecast connected to the back of the TV and the Google home app. You could also use Apple TV or a Telstra box. Find what suits your budget or use what you're used to using at home. Many caravan TVs are now smart TVs, so all you need is a Wifi connection.

Phone

We'll say it again: Telstra is the best choice for remote phone coverage. You will be surprised at how often you are using the internet while you travel. Finding dump points, water and supermarkets, researching tours and experiences, finding campsites and even posting on social media all chew up plenty of data, so make sure you don't leave yourself short on your mobile plan.

Cel-Fi Go

If having a good connection is imperative for your travels then a booster will help you achieve this. We have been using a Cel-Fi Go for a few years now and it can boost your single bar of 3G to full 3G, giving you much better reception. However, to use this you need some sort of reception in the first place—it's not a satellite phone and will not boost a signal in an area with no coverage.

Satellite phone

If you are travelling in areas with no reception, a satellite phone is a must. Not only does it give you peace of mind, it can save your life in emergencies or sticky situations.

Your first stop should be Facebook Marketplace or Gumtree for a second-hand phone, as many travellers purchase one for a trip and then sell it second-hand without having ever used it.

Although they are expensive, you can't really put a price on your safety and you will be thankful you have one in the unlikely event of an emergency.

They also can be used for happier or more everyday events: we have used one to call family to find out if they have had a new baby and Justin has called friends to get wind forecasts and information on how cyclones are tracking.

Washing

Having a washing machine on board is an absolute essential in our opinion. Why? Because you'll reach a point where you're forced to stay at a caravan park in order to wash. And at $5 per load, it's not exactly economical. The convenience of a washing machine in your caravan is priceless—even more so if you have one built in. This way you don't have to store it, pull it out and set it up to wash.

We have a 2kg Mini Daewoo washing machine and although it doesn't perform as well as a Fisher and Paykel washing machine, it's pretty good! We typically do three loads of washing every three days. Remember that on the road you'll find that if an item of clothing is 'cleanish', it goes back in the cupboard. An added bonus is that the kids spend half the trip in their swimmers or boardies. If you're travelling in warm conditions, you won't be washing bulky items, such as jumpers and jeans, very often. Get a washing machine— I promise, you'll thank us later!

We run a collapsible clothesline that we purchased from Anaconda and it fits our three loads of washing with extra room. We also utilise our permanent line on the awning, which is very handy not only for washing, but to air-dry towels and swimmers throughout the day.

All our dirty laundry is stored in a drawer or in the washing machine itself. However, in our last caravan we didn't have this space, so we would put our dirty clothes in a flexi tub to store in the shower.

Cleaning

Just because you're living on the road, doesn't mean the cleaning chores stop. With three kids at beach camps and with all that red dirt, our van has to be cleaned regularly. We have a broom and a Dyson handheld vacuum that I use every day!

To save space, we don't carry a mop. Instead, I get down on my hands and knees with Dettol wipes (and a bit of elbow grease) to clean the floors. This method isn't for everyone, but it works a treat and means we don't have to carry a mop. We use a spray and wipe to clean the shower and toilet and always carry mould killer—mould loves our shower.

For our toilet chemical we have used Boost, which can be purchased at Coles or Woolworths and costs about $4 for 1kg. It usually lasts a month and 1–2 scoops per canister load keeps the smell at bay. We've recently switched to a water-soluble sachet which eliminates the need for chemicals, meaning it's eco-friendly.

Best apps for travelling Australia

We have no affiliation with these apps, but they make up our essential digital toolkit and we recommend you look into making them part of yours.

WikiCamps Australia (\$7.99)

Your ultimate camping companion and our 'bible'. Works offline and is a database of campgrounds, national parks, free camps and caravan parks, as well as information on water points, dump points etc. A must-download.

Fuel Map Australia (free)

A crowd-sourced database of petrol stations and fuel prices across Australia. Comes with a handy fuel log so you can keep track of fuel purchases and your vehicle's fuel economy.

Camping
- WikiCamps (\$7.99)
- Campedia (\$1.99)
- Gas Finder (Refills & Swaps)
- Spirit level app of choice

Travelling/Driving
- Fuel Map Australia, or other fuel-finder app
- Hema 4WD Maps (\$69.99)

Budgeting
- Track My Tour
- TravelSpend

Weather
- Weatherzone
- Willy Weather

Health
- First Aid - Australian Red Cross
- F45 or other workout app/s of choice

Entertainment
- Spotify or other preferred music streaming app/s
- Netflix or other preferred content streaming app/s
- Apple Podcasts or other preferred app/s
- BorrowBox

Kids
- ABC Kids
- Aussie playground finder app of choice

Photo editing
- Adobe Lightroom
- InShot

Everything we wish we'd known before we started

1. Be patient while your family adjusts to van life. We promise it gets easier and you will fall in love with the travelling lifestyle.

2. Food—keep the basics stocked and shop as you go. Gone are the days you could do a huge shop at Aldi and buy everything in bulk. There just isn't enough storage for that. We keep the basics well-stocked and buy meat, fish, pasta and rice in bulk to keep costs down, then we shop regularly for fresh produce, milk and bread.

3. Cook big meals and freeze them—it is an easy option after a long day exploring. Pull your meal out of the freezer, pop it in the microwave and the kids are fed in a few minutes! Pasta bakes are a great freezer meal.

4. Storage is your best friend. We have plenty of good storage in our van and it makes life a whole lot easier. We have a good set-up in the back of our ute too, which is great for all the extra stuff you need when travelling the country. Storage ideas include caddies, tubs, lots of sticky dots and heavy duty double-sided tape.

5. You'll save loads of time and money by having your own on-board washing machine. At $4–5 per load in caravan parks, this otherwise becomes a real expense. Plus, waiting in line sucks.

6. An outdoor camp pantry/shelving is handy. We have stored shoes, bathers, towels, sunscreen and sand toys among other things. It's easily accessible and we just pop it in the doorway of the van while travelling.

7. Sturdy hooks are your best mate. Think hats, keys and bags! We go for the quality removable hooks as they are easily removed and don't damage your interior.

8. Investing in a decent handheld vacuum is essential. We have a Dyson and use it multiple times a day. There's no avoiding the fact that you'll get plenty of sand and red dust throughout your caravan.

9. When kitting out your beds with sheets and quilts, opt for darker colours such as grey. It hides the marks accumulated on your bed cover and the red dust from your (clean) feet. That stuff gets everywhere!

10. Rig up a permanent clothesline on your caravan. We run one across the length of our awning and it is very handy when doing small loads of washing or hanging up swimmers.

11. You can get away without having an oven in your van if you have a BBQ with a lid—just use it as an oven. Trust me, it does the job and does a mean cake or roast. It also provides a lot of extra storage in your kitchen area.

12. Quality gear doesn't come cheap but it is worth investing in good gear. When you're in the middle of nowhere, you'll be thankful you bought the decent stuff! Justin lives by the saying: 'A poor man buys twice.'

13. Don't put too many expectations on your trip, just go with the flow and everything will work out. We have learnt from experience that if you plan too much you will miss out on a lot of fun opportunities and experiences.

14. Get yourself an excellent mat for your door entry. We run a Muk Mat one.

15. Don't opt for hanging space in your cupboards, go with shelving as you just won't hang stuff.

16. If you love coffee, take a coffee machine. When you're remote and there are no cafes available, holy heck you'll want that machine.

17. If you're heading to the WA coast or Queensland, you'll be doing tonnes of snorkelling so look into buying decent snorkels for the family. We have used the Ninja Shark Mask and swear by it!

18. An onboard toilet is a must when travelling and toilet training. No one wants to walk a four-year-old over to the amenities at 3am.

19. Having a shower/bath recess in our caravan has been awesome. It means the kids can have a bath while you prepare dinner and watch the news. It's a win-win situation!

20. Storing drink bottle holders in the bunk beds means you don't have to get up through the night to get your child a drink of water. We bought cheap bike holder ones from Kmart for $8 each.

21. There is no day care to drop the kids to when you need a break—it's all us, so it can be full on at times. We do miss these breaks, as the day-care day was the perfect time to run errands without three kids in tow. We definitely make sure to schedule in 'mum and dad time' as well as solo time, because that is important too!

22. Do whatever it takes to keep little ones in their daytime sleep routine. When Charli was a baby she would still take a nap around lunch time every day. She became so well acquainted with life on the road that she could sleep anywhere: the car, the Ergo (baby carrier), the beach and even on a seesaw. A well-rested toddler is a happy little traveller!

23. Give the family a 'chill out' or rest day. We simply cannot head off exploring every day—it becomes exhausting!— and we love having days set aside to watch a movie or just hang out around the caravan. It's important as little ones cannot 'go go go' and need time to do their own thing.

24. When you first begin your travels, be as consistent as possible with your new routine and rules; it will eventually work in your favour. For us, it was getting all three kids down by 7pm in the triple bunks. Initially, there was loads of chatter and late bedtimes, which made for tired and grumpy gremlins the next day! Once they are used to the new sleeping arrangements, it gives Mum and Dad more time to chill out at night and enjoy dinner together, watch Netflix or work.

25. Toys are great to have on hand to diffuse arguments between our kids. Cheap $1 bubble wands are easy to store and entertaining for the kids in the middle of nowhere. Lego and craft have also been known to save the day.

26. Pop a box/tub at the end of your kids' beds. It keeps all their personal stuff (favourite Lego, pictures, school awards) in one spot, neat and tidy.

27. You might not like this one, but look into taking a device for your kids. It makes those long travel days much easier and can get you through another hour. And you'll probably also need it for schooling on the road.

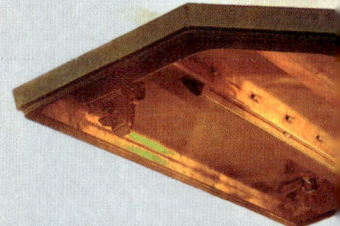

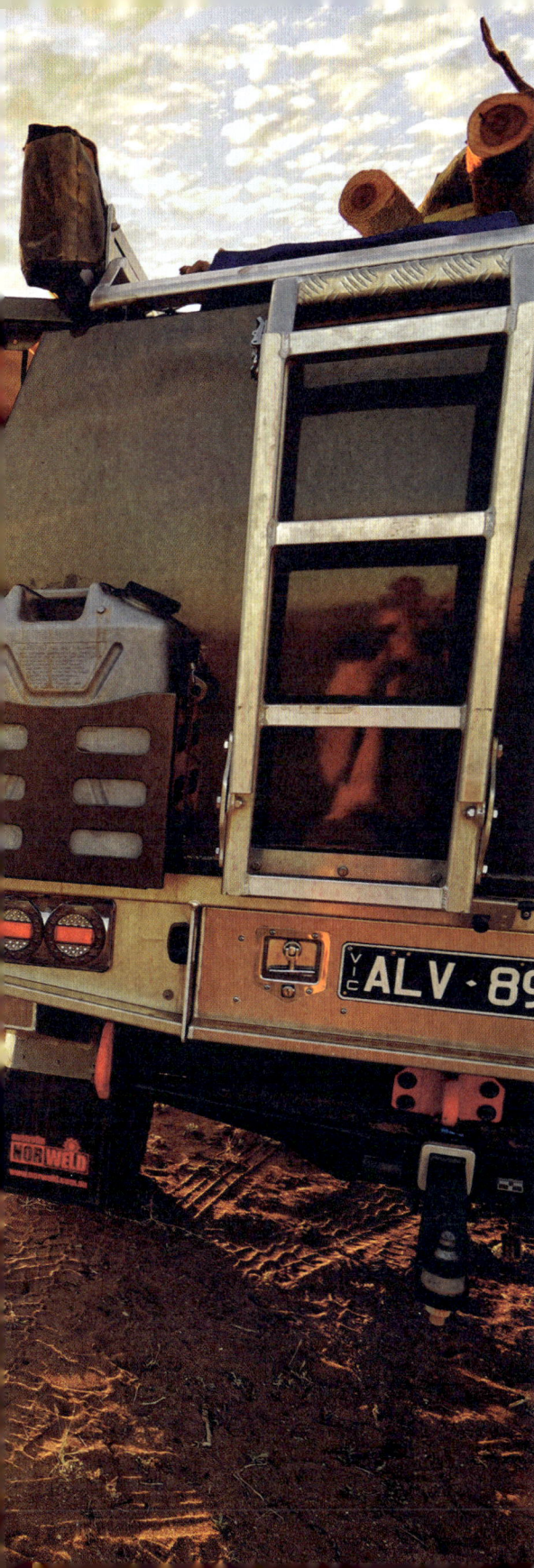

Free camping

If you feel daunted by free camping here are a few tips to get you started. Sometimes there is nothing better than pulling up into a secluded spot with no power or water taps in sight.

Free camping has two definitions. The first is self-sufficient camping, meaning you're staying somewhere that isn't an officially designated campground, with no power or water. The second is when designated campgrounds are completely free of charge but you are still self-sufficient camping.

Free camping sites around Australia are becoming rarer and rarer and the majority of good campsites are now 'low-cost'. Practising waterless and powerless camping in your driveway before you leave on your trip is a great way to test out your free camping capabilities, as figuring out how you will prepare your meals is just as important as knowing how your toilet and shower will function.

Grey water

A grey water tank is an extra tank fitted under your caravan into which you can divert and catch all your grey water. Grey water is all your drainage from your shower, sink and vanity.

Having a grey water tank is becoming much more common than it used to be as some campgrounds—particularly those in national parks—now require you to have one to stay. I do recommend you have one installed on your caravan, and you can even do this yourself!

Dump points

You will become well acquainted with dump points when you're travelling. It's not the loveliest of jobs, but for the convenience of having an onboard toilet, this quick job really isn't that bad! Dump points are located in plenty of towns around Australia and you won't have any trouble finding one.

Dump points are pinpointed on the WikiCamps app and you will see signs as you drive along the highway too.

Power and solar

In a nutshell, most caravans will need 12V power to free camp, so you will need to think about how much power your equipment will use prior to your camping trip.

Installing a good battery monitor with your 12-volt system is a great way to tell how your fridge, lights and appliances are running.

Your batteries can charge through the car alternator when you're driving, or through a generator (if permitted) or solar panels. To calculate the capacity your set-up requires for an overnight stopover, add the current draw of all the appliances you want to run. We use and recommend Enerdrive lithium battery systems.

Water and water fill points

Having the ability to carry lots of fresh water means you can free camp for longer in remote destinations. Water is precious, so be sure to test out how many days you can live off your onboard water tanks before heading off. Try to limit your collective daily usage to about 40 litres a day. Fast showers, doing the dishes once a day and not washing clothes are three great ways to save water. We think 300 litres of onboard water for a family is a good amount.

A water filter is also an excellent option and, in our opinion, essential when touring Australia—you don't want to be drinking any nasty water, trust us. We learnt that the hard way when we drank bad water in the Northern Territory and contracted a nasty bug which had us crook for nearly 6 weeks. We had to declare our situation to the NT and WA health departments after a blood test so they could track the problem back to the water source. Since then, we always have bottled water on hand when we head remote, in case we can't fill up our drinking water tanks with good water.

The lesson: don't drink bore water without boiling it and don't drink anything you feel unsure about.

Water fill points are everywhere and you really won't have any trouble filling your tanks. Again, the WikiCamps app is a godsend as not only does it help you locate campgrounds, it also lists the water points around the country. Information centres and service centres also generally have water fill points.

Security

Free camping in remote campsites around Australia can be daunting to many travellers—thanks in no small part to the movie *Wolf Creek*, I'm sure!

However, in seven years of travel our family has never felt unsafe. At times we have had a bad gut feeling which has seen us move on to another location. There are plenty of travellers on the road and it will be rare for you to pull into a camp and not see someone else around.

Our best advice is if you feel unsafe, move on. If you don't like travelling alone, check on forums for other travellers in the area. Plan to get to a camp early so you can suss it out before deciding to stay.

When leaving your caravan at a free camp to explore, it is essential that you feel your home and belongings are safe. Our tip is to take anything that is of worth with you. When tripping away from our caravan, we take our valuables with us and lock them in the ute's canopy.

We also use an alarm system called a WiTi, which gives us total peace of mind, as well as a trailer hitch lock. This is a motion-activated device that sets off an audible alarm and applies your trailer brakes to prevent theft.

Food, exercise and health

Food and meals

We eat really well while travelling and nothing about our diet has changed since we left home and embarked on our travels. We eat the same food and prepare the same meals as if we were living back in our home.

Travelling can be closely associated with happy hours, chips, dips and a snag on the barbie, but for us this is our lifestyle, so we eat healthily most days!

Having a decent size freezer is essential. Being able to bulk freeze pre-prepared meals is so important and enables you to pull a meal out of the freezer and have the kids fed in minutes. Having prepared meals to quickly heat up after a big day exploring definitely makes for a stress-free dinner.

We like to make up big batches of pasta bake, zucchini slice, tuna bake or spaghetti bol and pop them into the freezer. We pack meals into Ziplock bags so they lie flat, which maximises room in the freezer. Containers aren't really an option for your caravan-size freezer.

When you're driving long distances, good food is key! We make up a snack and lunch bag for each family member. This eliminates the urge to buy garbage food at the servo or swing through McDonald's. It's expensive to eat takeaway while travelling and you wouldn't believe the money some families spend in a month doing so. So, stick with a sandwich and some fruit.

After all, your home is right behind you and making lunch from scratch has never been so convenient.

Groceries

One of our biggest costs while travelling Australia is the grocery bill for our family of five.

Our grocery budget hovers around $450–$500 per week, depending on the location; being remote without access to the big chain supermarkets makes a huge difference.

We eat pretty well. It's important to us to have a balance of good foods and give our three kids all the proper nutrition they need. I'm no expert, I just want them fuelled with the good stuff! Our kids don't cope very well on preservatives and sugar so I try to avoid these as much as possible.

One of the most common questions we are asked is what we eat while travelling. Here is a breakdown for you . . .

TRIP IN A VAN

Healthy food ideas

Breakfast

- Porridge (quick oats cost $1.10 for a 750g bag—they're a bargain and they keep tummies full)
- Scrambled eggs
- Baked beans on toast
- Smoothies (we have a Nutribullet)
- Bacon and eggs
- Cereals and fruit

Lunch

- Sandwiches
- Chicken and salad wraps
- Tuna and avocado on rice cakes
- Tuna and brown rice
- Protein shakes

Snacks—adults

- Fruit
- Muesli bars
- Nuts
- Coffee (we have a coffee machine)
- Boiled eggs
- Rice cakes
- Smoothies

Snacks—kids

- LOADS of fruit—watermelon, grapes, apples, bananas and mandarins are staples
- Muesli bars or no-bake healthy bars (homemade)
- Rice Wheels
- Ryvitas
- Rice cakes
- Popcorn
- Peanut butter on Cruskits
- Boiled eggs

Dinner—adults

- Steak and veg
- Chicken stir-fries
- Fish (caught) and salad
- Mini roasts
- Curries
- Tacos
- Tofu and salad
- Camp oven stews and roasts

Dinner—kids

- Tuna bake
- Zucchini slice
- Spaghetti bolognese
- Fish and salad
- Snags/chicken and vegies
- Ravioli and vegies
- Tuna and brown rice
- Quiche
- Meatloaf
- Curry
- Tacos

Exercise

We are often asked how we manage to maintain our fitness and stay active while we travel. It is really important to us that we stay fit, healthy and happy, both mentally and physically.

Keeping up with three kids and hiking, swimming, snorkelling, bike riding and our general lifestyle means we're very active! That said, it's still important for us to work out and we feel at our absolute best when we stick to a regular routine.

Every time we go for a run, to the gym, or to do some stairs, we always come back fresher. It's a great escape from the kids, plus it teaches them the importance of exercise. We do enjoy attending gyms and our favourite workout is an F45 class.

When we can, we sign up for a week at F45—though I wouldn't recommend this if you're sticking to a tight budget as it is expensive. You'll find that most towns you pass through will have some kind of gym with short-term visit options.

The rest of the time, we do HIIT workouts together under our awning using an app. DIY workouts using apps are an affordable and convenient option. There are so many to choose from, such as Centr, Sweat by Kayla Itsines or F45.

Justin and I aim to do a 20-minute HIIT workout every second day. On our off days, we jog, go for a walk or have a rest day—just find something you love and stick to it.

We use resistance bands for strength and conditioning as this mimics the free weight exercises we'd be doing in a gym. Plus, they're lightweight and take up no room in our van.

Health

Staying healthy while travelling is extremely important! No one wants to pick up a vomiting bug and have it go through the whole family (trust me, we've been there).

Drinking bottled water in remote areas is vital in order to avoid water-borne bacteria. A 24-pack of bottled water from Woolworths is as little as $6, so we recommend keeping this on hand and getting a water filter fitted to your caravan. If you do become unwell and need a doctor urgently, it's usually best to head to the local hospital. They are very accommodating of travellers as they know it can be near impossible to get into a doctor as a 'new patient'. If you're a long way from a hospital, and on a traveller's budget like us, try to find a bulk-billing doctor—a quick Google search of 'bulk billing dr near me' usually does the trick. There are also now app services if you require a doctor's appointment via video call. I have used and can recommend Instant Consult.

We keep a box of medications on hand as well as a first aid kit and snake bite kit. These are an absolute must when you're travelling in remote areas. Be mindful of what you eat and drink and don't put off seeing a doctor if you're unwell.

Most importantly, make sure you have ambulance cover that covers you Australia wide. It's very affordable and you can pay a yearly upfront fee with your state. If you're a Queenslander all you need is a driver's licence and you're covered. It's also worth checking your health insurance policy if you have one, as most include some level of ambulance cover.

Earning on the road

Ways to fund the dream: SAVE, SAVE, SAVE

If you have enough money behind you to last the duration of your trip, you beauty! We saved $52,000 to financially support us for a year so we didn't have to find work. Many save for years to make this happen and everyone's financial situation is different.

Use maternity leave or long service leave

Just had a baby or have long service leave? Why not use that income and travel Australia? If you have bulk leave banked up, consider working that into your travels, as it will give you a reduced weekly wage but will spread your income out over a longer period of time.

Work remotely

We have met many travellers who have taken their job remote, or scaled back from full time. It can be doable with a phone and laptop depending on your field of work. You'll never know if you don't ask . . .

Rent

A fantastic way to fund your travels is to rent your home out. If you are in a position to do so, go for it. We know families who rent their home out for $1000 a week, which covers the cost of their travel and allows them to come home to a place they love after their trip.

Make a call to your local real estate agency for advice on the rental market and potential income from tenants.

Sell up

We know plenty of families who have sold their home to fund their travel set-up, but this wasn't for us. We preferred to save and keep our house money set aside for when we decide to settle and purchase a home again. Each to their own—do what is right for you.

Pick up work along the way

There are loads of families currently travelling who are picking up work along the way, either in their field of work or something completely different, such as fruit picking, campground caretaking or other odd jobs. Check out my list of Facebook groups that can help you pick up work on the road (see page 50).

Take your business remote

Do you work in the online sector? You're well placed to take your business on the road. Even if you have an established business, it's still possible to work remotely. We met a family with a successful earthmoving business who employed someone to run the day-to-day stuff while they were on hand via the phone if needed. They handled invoicing and the finance side of the business from their van. We've met people running a recruiting business from their caravan three days a week and exploring and travelling the rest of the week. In the post-pandemic age of remote working, this is becoming more and more common.

Use your skills or trade

If you have a trade or are skilled in other ways, there are plenty of opportunities to pick up work around the country. We have met loads of families who have stopped for a month or two in mining areas to top up the bank account.

If you're a nurse there are so many remote jobs via agencies that pay really well. And if you're a teacher, hairdresser or barista, there is work out there for you. Gumtree is a great place to search for jobs in your area of travel.

We've seen it all: yoga instructors, personal trainers, jewellery makers—you can make money while travelling, whether that's by setting up a stall at the local markets or popping a sign out the front of your van in a caravan park to do haircuts.

Making money through blogging and social media

I'll be honest: when you're starting out, online travel content means a lot of work for very little return.

We now have a social media following behind us to push traffic to our website and content. But if you want to give it a crack because you have a real passion, go for it—just know you need to be in it for the long haul and you'd probably make more money by stopping for a stint to work!

Social media

Having a travel diary on social media is fun and a great way to meet new people and other families and couples travelling Australia. For us, what started out as a way to keep people in the loop eventually became our job. Our only advice: don't set out to become a social influencer. Have fun, spend time with your family and experience as much as you can—because after all, that is the reason you set off on a road trip in the first place. However, if you enjoy posting your pics and have a flair for photography and video, then have fun with it. But always, always remember to keep the balance and don't let it take away from your trip.

We have met lots and lots of families through this platform and some have become our greatest friends, so we are thankful for that little app.

Groups to add yourself to:

- Working While Living on the Road
- Outback Jobs in Australia
- Station Positions in Northern Australia
- Farm Work Australia
- Working as we Travel
- Australian Rural and Remote Jobs
- Nurses on the Road Travelling Australia
- Workout Australia
- Working on the Road Australia
- Station/Farming Jobs Australia
- Farm Jobs Australia
- Australia Fruit Picking/Packing/Solar Farms
- Fruit Picking Jobs
- Grey Nomad Jobs
- Teachers On The Road Travelling Australia
- Short Term Bush Jobs for Travelling Tradesmen - Australia

Travelling with kids

Raising kids on the road

Travelling with three kids can obviously have its moments. However, they are now well adjusted to living on the road full-time. They thrive on the ever-changing destinations and constant adventure. From our time on the road, we've seen many changes in our little ones and they've hit plenty of milestones. Travelling has boosted their confidence, learning and social interactions. Their swimming is fantastic and they've developed resilient, outgoing personalities. I love that they're climbing trees, making sandcastles and playing with sticks and stones.

Living on the road is a lifestyle, and routine and structure are important. It's crucial for them to acknowledge when the day starts and ends, when we have downtime and of course the dinner, bath, bedtime rituals. It reduces the tantrums and tiredness, making our days and our adventures run much more smoothly.

Being in a confined space can have the best of us getting anxious. So how do we handle this with kids on board? In all honesty, we're hardly ever stuck in the van for long periods of time. We're out exploring, snorkelling, hiking and making memories. The kids are forever occupied or they entertain themselves, a fantastic skill they've learnt while travelling. They're happy to climb a tree, ride bikes and make potions.

As challenging as our dynamic home can be at times, it sure beats dealing with all the same challenges in a static home. Plus I have the added bonus of having my husband around full-time—another parent to help with the chaos!

In a nutshell, I remind myself that we live a lifestyle that many envy and we are on the ride of a lifetime. Spending all this time with our kids (as difficult as it can be at times) caravanning around Australia is an opportunity to really get to know them, love them and be there for them in ways many other parents cannot be.

Our tips for travelling with kids

Routine

Try and keep your kids in a routine as best you can, especially the little ones. This is particularly critical when you're schooling your kids remotely.

Involve your kids in the planning of your trip

Our kids love talking about upcoming destinations and the activities ahead. It's also great to prepare them for car travel the day before so it's not a surprise that they will be sitting in the car for over 500km.

Your house on wheels

I recommend getting a caravan to suit your family's needs. For us that means a shower and a toilet. I wasn't keen on the idea of getting three kids under four into the amenities to shower them every night, and toilet training is so much easier in your caravan!

Pre-cook meals

After a big day exploring, there's nothing worse than getting back to your van late and having to organise dinner for hungry kids. This is why I keep ready-made meals in the freezer.

To sum it all up

Parent your own way—we definitely won't judge you. Figure out how to keep it together, get your 'me time', and grab a solo coffee to cope, but also remember to have a drink and fist pump the air when you're having a parenting win. This is a pretty sweet parenting gig and the opportunity of a lifetime that you'll treasure forever!

Travelling with kids on long car travel days

'Are we there yet?' is a pretty common phrase from kids when you are travelling long distances. Every parent can agree that it is frustrating! So how do you keep the kids entertained over long distances?

Some days you'll nail it and others are a nightmare. Just go with it! We have done plenty of car travel with our kids and a big day for us is usually around 500km.

Make sure you are prepared. You never want to go into a long travel day without charged iPads and plenty of snacks. Take the drive as an opportunity to do some schoolwork or listen to kid-friendly podcasts

We like to hit the road by 9am—it's a bonus if we are in the car earlier. Our rule is no iPads in the first hour. This means we all get to chat and the kids pick their favourite music to play. We have our healthy snacks in the car and a full water bottle each and we smash out the first 300km. Then we find a park, playground or rest stop and pull over for an hour while we have lunch and let the kids burn off some energy.

Then it's back in the car for the remainder of the trip and the kids will watch a movie. This enables us to get to our destination in the early afternoon, before dark. It also means the kids have a few hours to run around before dinner and bed.

When our kids were younger, we would time our car travel with nap times and do the majority of our driving then. This is what worked for us, time and time again, but you will find what works for your family. Practice makes perfect!

Homeschooling

Schooling on the road can seem pretty daunting, and as a parent, you're usually delving into a world of the unknown! I sure was—but after talking to all the travelling mums out there I soon realised that educating your kids on the road is surprisingly doable.

My first bit of advice is that the schooling stream you decide to go with really depends on the child and parent. You know your child best—their strengths and weaknesses and how they will learn best. Do your research, ask around, ask their teachers and put questions forward in online groups on Facebook.

There are plenty of options out there: homeschooling, distance education, unschooling (where students' education is not dictated by a curriculum) and School of the Air.

Research them all. If you're off on a twelve-month lap, you need to have the right education provider to make schooling your children seamless. I do want to point out here that it's not always easy. Some days are hectic and others are a breeze—just take it as it comes and stay patient and consistent with schooling. We began with homeschooling prep. Although we coped for most of the year through resources such as Reading Eggs, IXL Maths, sight words and workbooks, our son grew bored and I just didn't have the resources I needed to keep him engaged.

In Year 1 we moved to distance education and this is by far what works best for our family. We started with a school called NEPSODE—North East Public School Of Distance Education—which is based in Port Macquarie, and we have since moved on to SIDE—School of Isolated and Distance Education.

It's also worth talking to your current school, as they may be happy to keep your child enrolled and send or email resources to you.

How do we receive materials?

Our schooling resources arrive in the mail every month. The package contains a USB which has online lessons and video tutorials on whatever the kids are learning or are required to learn as part of the school curriculum, along with readers, craft and worksheets. We also have access to online lessons the kids can participate in.

How much work is involved?

I am impressed with the schoolwork we are sent, and it has kept our kids really engaged. It's so appropriate for their interests and academic level. The work is packed in a folder, along with about ten readers (which are tailored to their interests), craft, MAB blocks for maths and clicking blocks, among other things.

With the workload set out by their teacher, we aim to do about 1½ hours of schoolwork five days a week. They also have a non-compulsory live lesson with their teacher once a week which goes for about an hour. If needed, we play catch up from the week over the weekend if we have been busy exploring, but usually we have no problem getting through the work. If you think about how much time in a classroom is chewed up by organisation, admin and play, it's actually a very manageable workload for a homeschooled child.

Utilise libraries and museums, as they are fantastic places to take the kids. We love to stop in at libraries and do puzzles, or some reading and colouring in.

Our kids have developed an amazing amount of resilience, and they're extremely social, capable and adaptable. What I love is that they're willing to give anything a crack and do things well beyond their young years. They not only adapt to all situations and take everything in their stride, they're well balanced and open-minded. Our kids are not only learning academically but learning important life skills.

Healthy food ideas for kids on the go

When you're on the go, it can be hard to keep kids fuelled with the good stuff and to steer clear of the nasties.

I love the health food aisle. Healtheries Rice Wheels are a hit with the kids. I can chuck them in my backpack and grab them out on top of a mountain. Another option is Messy Monkey Wholegrain Bites—I rate the burger ring flavour. Delish! Mini Bites are a great snack too.

Popcorn is always a winner—healthy and nutritious and it comes in a generous size bag (good for adults too). I usually purchase the Freedom Food or Sam's Pantry muesli bars and the kids love them as a mid-morning snack after a beach swim. Be wary when purchasing muesli bars though; some are packed with sugar and preservatives.

Fruit—we can't keep up with demand. From bananas to apples and grapes, watermelon, strawberries, blueberries and mangoes, it's by far the best snack. Cut it up into bite-sized pieces or make apple chips with peanut butter. A fruit salad with yoghurt is a good option too.

Rice cakes come in all varieties now. Our go-tos are cheese or spring onion. I always have a packet at my feet in the car and they don't last long. Sakatas and Peckish come in little packets now and they're super handy when you're on the move. We also love Cruskits with peanut butter and honey.

Prunes, dates and apricots are good options; we call them 'lollies' and the kids think they're getting a treat! Some do contain preservatives so go organic where you can. Our three kids also love canned tuna for a tasty snack while on the go.

Carrot and celery sticks are always a success, and team them with some hummus or peanut butter and the kids are stoked. Baked beans in a can are always handy but be sure you don't forget a spoon. We change things up with bliss balls and organic corn chips every now and then.

If you've got a fridge in the back of your car, yoghurt is a fantastic snack to have with you. When travelling with a baby, we always had this on hand and kept a 'hangry' baby happy. Boiled eggs are another one of our favourites—they keep for a few days and stay stocked up in our fridge. Pop a little bit of salt and pepper on them and the adults will love them too.

If you're feeling a little creative, zucchini slice is delicious and our kids eat this hot or cold. We also make breakfast muffins, pancakes, pasta spirals, sushi and 'clean' baked bars and slices. Oh, I could go on!

Our biggest tip is to stay away from processed food and snacks containing sugar (or large amounts of it, anyway). There's nothing worse than a kid on a sugar high when you've got a day driving 500km!

Travelling with a partner

A note from Bec

I know, I know, you absolutely love your family and couldn't be without them. But being with each other every single day of every week without a break to catch up with friends, grab some alone time or even go to work. . . Look, it can be tough.

Communication is absolutely key and being honest enough to tell your husband he's being an arse can actually be a useful tactic. If you find your loved one is frustrated and anxious, or being short with the kids, get him out of there. Send him fishing, for a drive or on a bike ride around camp. He'll come back a new man, a better dad, and before you know it he'll be farting on their heads

again. It's a huge adjustment for everyone being around each other all the time, and we need time out now and again.

Mum needs her downtime too. So tell your husband when you need some time out, and go and grab a coffee, or head off to chat to that mum you've seen around the campground. However you decide to do it, take some quality time for yourself.

Have each other's backs, stay on the same page and before you know it, you'll be taking it all in and loving your once-in-a-lifetime trip, making awesome memories.

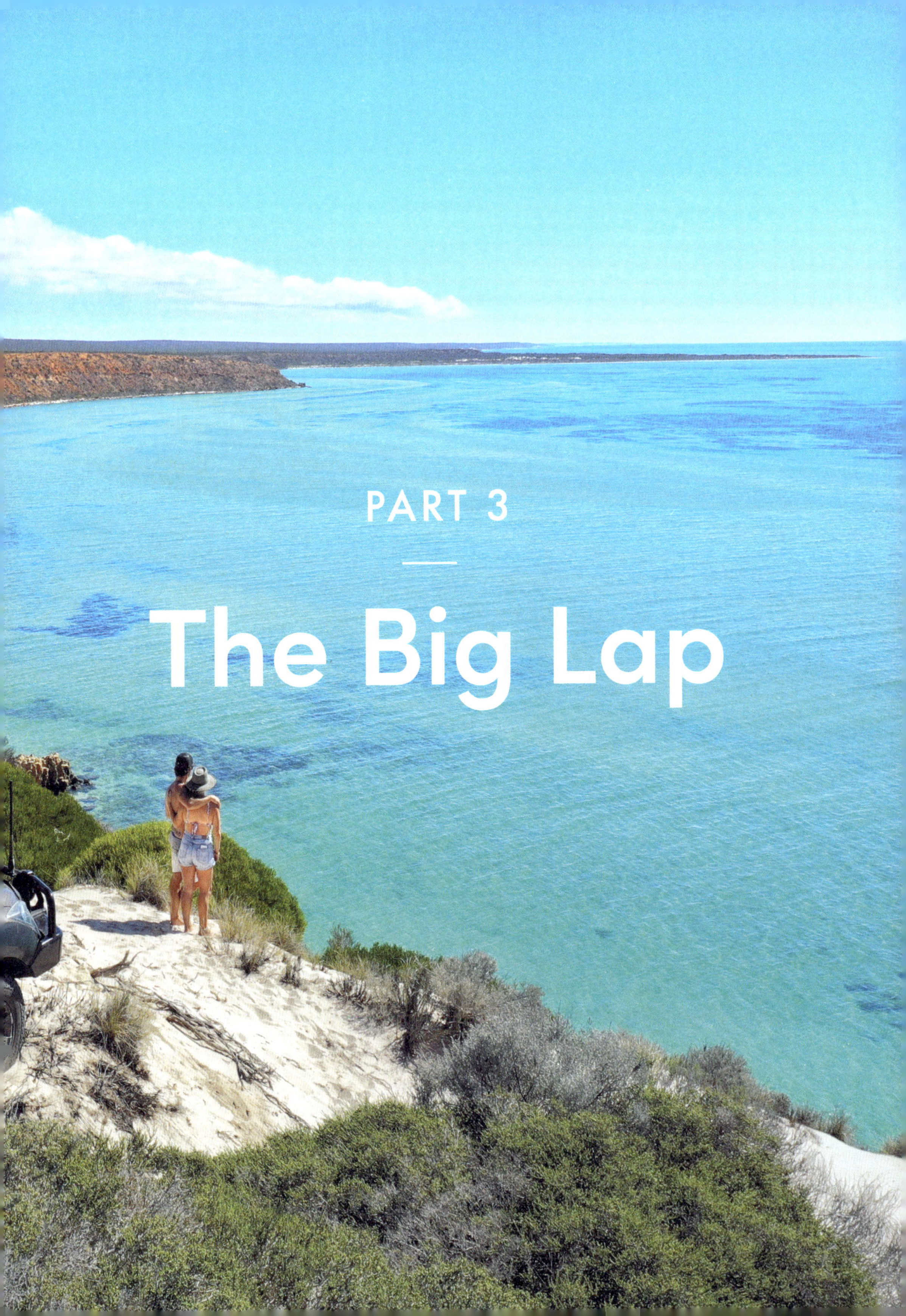

PART 3

The Big Lap

The ultimate lap of Australia

This is the complete guide, created by us! It provides you with all the best destinations around Australia to explore and covers the must-do activities and attractions in each area. This itinerary has a bit of everything: caravan parks, free camps, national parks and low-cost camps. We urge you to experience all types of camping to really immerse yourself in the diversity and landscapes of Australia.

We've also included the best coffee in some of these destinations, because no one likes a rubbish coffee. These places come tried and tested by us.

We've taken the stress and time out of researching where to stay and knowing you'll be parked up somewhere safe and enjoyable on your big lap. We'd advise making the small investment to get yourself a yearly membership through BIG4 and/or the Discovery Parks G'day Rewards Program.

Another fantastic membership is the TAWK (Travel Australia With Kids) which gets you two nights free for kids at designated caravan parks and some free activities.

Consider a national parks pass, which you can purchase in each state. Be mindful that this does not cover some of the most popular parks such as Monkey Mia, which charge additional fees.

In some destinations your only option is to stay at a caravan park. Booking an unpowered site over a powered site will save you money.

Note: We are in no way affiliated with these caravan parks, campsites, attractions and activities. These are from our own personal experience and this is 100% OUR advice only. If you come across a campsite or caravan park that is disappointing, has closed down or has changed in some way from our review, we would love to know. We'd like to continue improving and updating this itinerary. Please email us at tripinavan@gmail.com. Thank you!

KEY

☼ ATTRACTIONS

🛖 CARAVAN PARK

⛺ FREE OR LOW-COST CAMPING

☕ COFFEE/FOOD

TRIP IN A VAN

——

Victoria

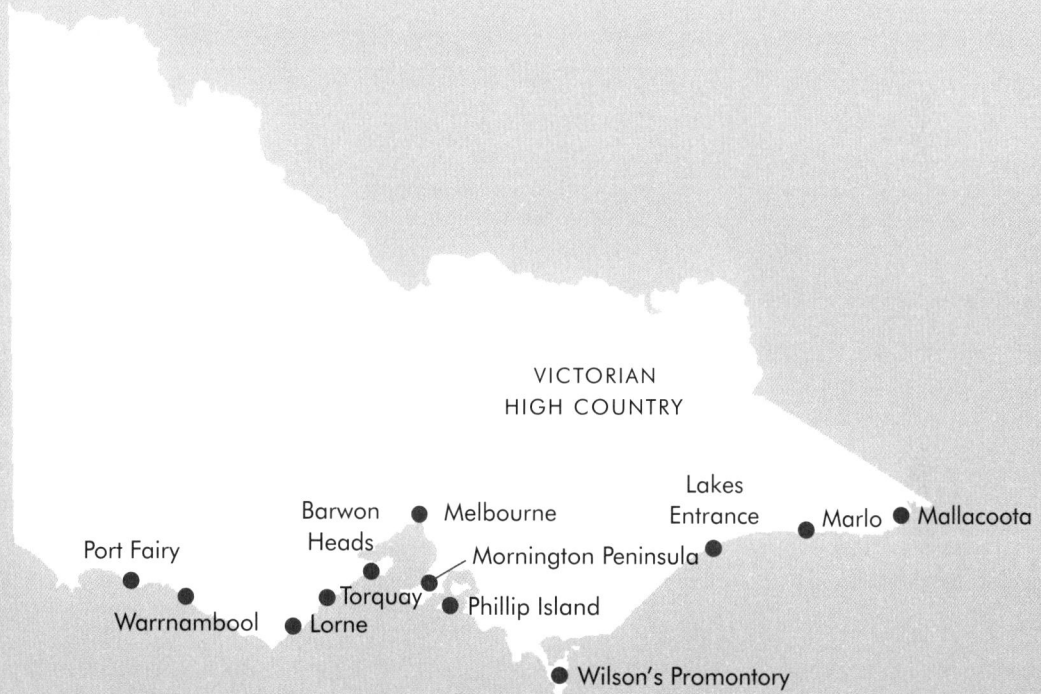

VICTORIAN
HIGH COUNTRY

Barwon
Heads

Melbourne

Lakes
Entrance

Marlo

Mallacoota

Port Fairy

Mornington Peninsula

Torquay

Phillip Island

Warrnambool

Lorne

Wilson's Promontory

Mallacoota

A small town surrounded by beautiful beaches and stunning wilderness. The village, which is situated on the Mallacoota inlet, has an element of remoteness but is very popular with holidaymakers and families.

☼ Fishing, swimming, stand-up paddleboarding

🚐 Mallacoota Foreshore Holiday Park

⛺ Genoa Camp Park

Marlo

Surrounded by bush and farmland, Marlo is nestled on the mouth of the Snowy River. A sleepy seaside town.

☼ River and ocean swimming, fishing

🚐 Marlo Ocean View Caravan Park

⛺ Snowy Riverside, Newmerella

Lakes Entrance

A seaside town with a man-made channel that consists of a unique system of stunning waterways. A popular destination for young families.

☼ Buchan Caves, Ninety Mile Beach

🚐 NRMA Eastern Beach Holiday Park

⛺ Waterwheel Beach Tavern—Lake Tyers Beach, Log Crossing—Kalimna, Tostaree Cottages and Farmstay

Wilsons Promontory

As Victoria's oldest national park, it attracts hundreds of thousands of visitors every year and for good reason! Also home to the southernmost tip of the Australian mainland.

☼ Wildlife, Squeaky Beach, Mt Oberon summit walk, Norman Bay

🚐 Tidal River Camping and Caravan Site

⛺ Tidal River Camping and Caravan Site

Phillip Island

A fantastic seaside destination full of activity, wildlife, beaches and the V8 Supercars.

☼ Cape Woolamai, Phillip Island Penguin Parade, Nobbies Centre

🚐 Cowes Caravan Park, Amaroo Holiday Park

🥤 Island Wholefoods—Cowes

Mornington Peninsula

With amazing clifftop walks and drives, the peninsula is a mix of urban areas, resort towns and rural farming land. Stunning beaches, produce, wineries and loads more to explore.

☼ Wineries, Cape Schanck Lighthouse, Peninsula Hot Springs, Frankston Foreshore Precinct, The Big Goose

🚐 BIG4 Mornington Peninsula Holiday Park Frankston, Kangerong Holiday Park

⛺ Point Leo Beach Reserve, Whitecliffs Foreshore Camping

BELLS BEACH

Melbourne

A mix of style, sport, culture and arts. Noted as the world's most liveable city, it really is an exciting place to visit!

☼ Southbank and the Yarra River, Crown Casino precinct, Federation Square, Queen Victoria Markets, St Kilda Esplanade, Brighton Beach, Skydeck, Luna Park, Melbourne Aquarium

🚐 Melbourne BIG4 Holiday Park

Barwon Heads

This popular holiday town is located on the Barwon River. It has an old-world charm and a vibrant atmosphere. Enjoy a slower pace in this cosy beachside town.

☼ Sightsee Ocean Grove and Queenscliff, Barwon Heads Bluff, stand-up paddleboarding, surfing, swimming, Adventure Park Geelong, Bellarine Railway

🚐 Barwon Heads Caravan Park (kids free)

☕ Culture Coffee van

Victorian High Country

The Victorian High Country has the highest mountains in the state, plus a historically rich landscape of lakes, snow resorts and vineyards. The huts and campgrounds are spectacular and if you're keen to leave the van and hit the swags, some of the 4WD tracks and campsites are a lot of fun. Alternatively, you can camp in Bright and do day trips. Check out our website and YouTube for more detailed information!

☼ Craigs Hut, Billy Goat Track, Mansfield, Bright, Lovicks Hut, Bindaree Falls, Herns Spur Track, Dargo Hotel, Talbotville, Blue Rag Track, The Trigg

Torquay

The beginning of the Great Ocean Road and home to the famous Bells Beach. The town has an iconic surfing culture, great shopping, beautiful beaches and excellent eateries.

☼ Australian National Surfing Museum, Bells Beach, Jan Juc

🚐 Torquay Foreshore Caravan Park, Torquay Holiday Park

Lorne

A popular destination for holidaymakers and a picturesque town with plenty of atmosphere. Beautiful beaches and an arts community.

- Erskine Falls, Teddy's Lookout, Cumberland Falls, Lorne Sea Baths, Pier and Swing Bridge
- Lorne Foreshore Caravan Park, Cumberland River Holiday Park
- Big Hill Track Campground (seasonal), Bush n Beach Private House Camp—Aireys Inlet

Apollo Bay

In the stunning Otway Ranges, a scenic area with beautiful beaches.

- Cape Otway Lighthouse, Mariners Lookout, Mait's Rest, Anglesea
- BIG4 Apollo Bay Pisces Holiday Park, Wye River Beachfront Campground
- Johanna Beach, The Dairy Apollo Bay

LORNE

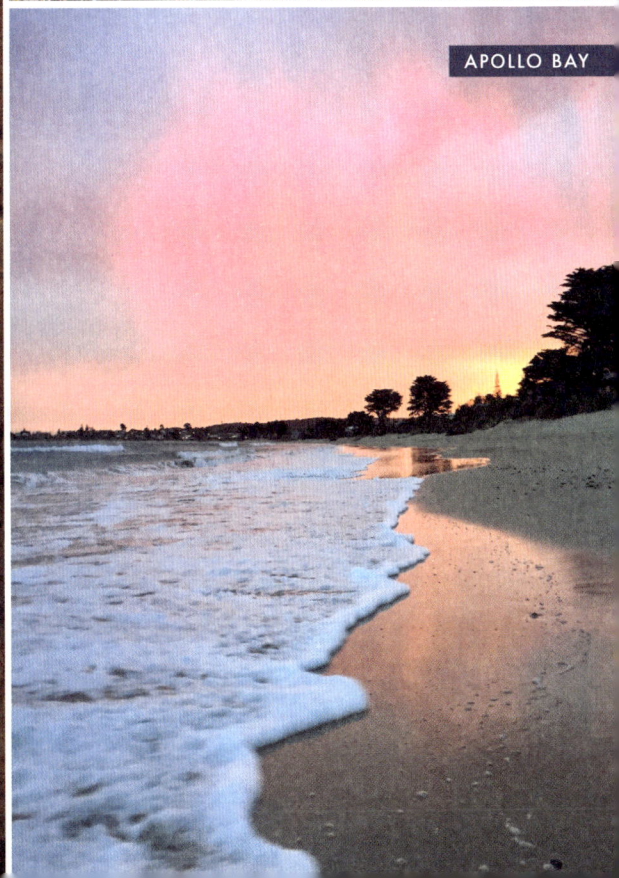

APOLLO BAY

Port Campbell

An iconic destination on the Great Ocean Road, famed for its sightseeing.

☼ Twelve Apostles, Loch Ard Gorge, London Bridge, The Arch, The Grotto, Bay of Martyrs

🚐 NRMA Port Campbell Holiday Park

⛺ Port Campbell Recreation Reserve

Warrnambool

A pretty former port city well known for its whale watching and for the movie *Oddball*. Shopping, cafes and attractions to keep the kids entertained. Plus, it's where Bec was born and spent her childhood.

☼ Lake Pertobe, Logans Beach whale watching, Flagstaff Hill, Tower Hill, meet the maremma dogs, Penguin and Middle Islands

🚐 Shipwreck Bay Holiday Park

⛺ Panmure Hotel, Panmure Free Camp

☕ Main Beach Kiosk, Rough Diamond

Port Fairy

A charming fishing village loaded with history. Beautiful beaches and a laid-back culture.

☼ Pea Soup Beach, Griffiths Island and Lighthouse, stroll the streets, Yambuk Slide

🚐 Port Fairy Holiday Park, BIG4 Port Fairy

☕ Bank Street Co.

GREAT OCEAN ROAD

HISTORICAL MARKER

South Australia

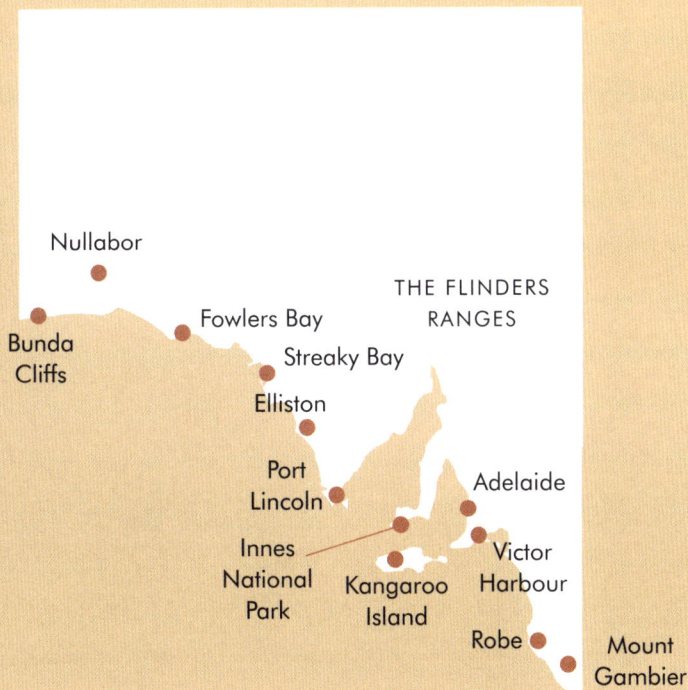

Nullabor

THE FLINDERS
RANGES

Bunda
Cliffs

Fowlers Bay

Streaky Bay

Elliston

Port
Lincoln

Adelaide

Innes
National
Park

Kangaroo
Island

Victor
Harbour

Robe

Mount
Gambier

BLUE LAKE

UMPHERSTON SINKHOLE

Mount Gambier

Located on the slopes of a volcanic landscape, this popular tourist destination is worth a stop for its natural attractions.

- Blue Lake, Umpherston Sinkhole, Big Lobster
- BIG4 Blue Lake Holiday Park, Pine Country Caravan Park
- Mt Gambier Showgrounds
- Bay Blue Espresso Bay, Presto Eatery

Robe

Amazing beaches and fishing and a town centre rich in history. A charming spot with boutique shopping, four-wheel drive tracks and a marina.

- 4WD up Long Beach, Little Dip Conservation Park, heritage buildings, Beachport, wineries
- Sea-Vu Caravan Park
- Mahalia Coffee

Kingston South East

Kingston SE has a low-cost campground by the beach and adjacent to the jetty. The Lions Park offers toilets, a dump point and a large area where you can pull up. Don't miss the lovely sunsets.

- Jetty and squid fishing, swimming, bike riding on the bike track along the beach

Victor Harbour

A popular coastal town with clifftop trails, large sandy beaches, bikeways and opportunities for marine life encounters.

- Horse-drawn Tram to Granite Island, SA Whale Centre, Port Elliott
- NRMA Victor Harbour Beachfront Holiday Park
- Port Elliott Showground, Breakaway Farmstay—Waitpinga, Bird Haven Retreat—Inman Valley

Kangaroo Island

There's loads to see and do on this remote and rugged island, from wineries to unusual rock formations. You'll be sure to have an adventure here!

☼ Remarkable Rocks, Admirals Arch, Seal Bay and boardwalk, Little Sahara for tobogganing, Dudley Wines cellar door

🚐 Western KI Caravan Park

⛺ American River Camping Ground, Emu Bay Campsite, Rocky River Campground, Vivonne Bay Campground

KANGAROO ISLAND

Rapid Bay

A low-cost beachfront campground with a jetty. Unpowered only, with amazing views and calm waters. Playground for the kids available.

☼ Rapid Bay Cove Cave, jetty fishing, swimming, Second Valley for scenery and swimming

Adelaide

Adelaide is a bustling city set on a stunning coastline. Well known for its stylish architecture, beautiful beaches, unique history, world-class events and exceptional food and wine.

☼ Hahndorf, Glenelg Beach, Adelaide Zoo, Melba's Chocolate Factory, Aerial Adventure Park, Cleland Wildlife & Conservation Park, Port Noarlunga, Aldinga Beach

🚐 BIG4 West Beach Parks

Point Turton

A peaceful seaside town with calm waters, Point Turton is an increasingly popular holiday destination.

☼ Jetty fishing, day trip to Innes National Park, pontoon jumping, snorkelling, ocean pools and Flaherty's Beach

🚐 Point Turton Caravan Park

⛺ Len Barker Reserve

RAPID BAY

POINT TURTON

WEST BEACH, ADELAIDE

Innes National Park

Well known for its spectacular coastal landscapes and rugged cliffs. The sandy beaches have great surf too. Camping is in the national park.

☼ Fishing, surfing, bushwalking, Pondalowie surf break, rock pools at Shell Beach, Stenhouse Bay & Jetty

🚐 Pondalowie Bay Campground, Gym Beach

Wauraltee Beach

A campground with a view and fires permitted. A stunning place to park up, though permits are required.

☼ Swimming, hiking, fishing and boating

Moonta Bay

Its amazing beaches, jetty and fishing make this town a big drawcard for families. The beautiful calm waters, splash park and overall atmosphere are sensational.

☼ Moonta Splash Park, Moonta Bay Jetty, squid fishing, Moonta Mines Railway

🚐 Moonta Bay Caravan Park

⛺ Moonta RV Overnight Stop Area

🥤 The Coffee Barn & Gelateria

Horrocks Pass Bush Camp

A free campground located on the way into the Flinders Ranges. Suitable for camper trailers and off-road caravans. Campfires allowed; no facilities.

FLINDERS RANGES

Willow Springs

Willow Springs is a great spot to base yourselves while exploring the Flinders Ranges. For more of the ranges see pages 90–92.

☼ Wilpena Pound, Skytrek Track, Stokes Hill Lookout at sunset, Alligator Gorge, Mount Remarkable National Park

🚐 Willow Springs, Wilpena Pound Resort

⛺ Willow Springs, Uppalina Station, national park campgrounds

From the Flinders Ranges, you can continue up the guts of Central Australia (see page 89) or down to the Eyre Peninsula (see page 101) or across the Nullarbor (see page 117).

—

Up the guts of Central Australia:

Port Augusta to Uluru

NT

Uluru

Kulgera Roadhouse

SA

Coober Pedy

Coward Springs

Mount Little Station

Port Augusta

BLUE RANGE WARREN GORGE

A private property run by a fantastic couple. There are plenty of campsites to choose from by the creek bed or within the gorge itself. Try spotting an endangered yellow-footed rock-wallaby or take a stroll through the gorge. Bring some wood in for a campfire and cook-up.

Distance: 60km from Port Augusta

Road type: Dirt track once you leave the highway

MOUNT LITTLE STATION

A sensational station located in the Flinders Ranges. Your first stop is the homestead where you'll meet the wonderful owners who will kindly give you a map, directions and a list of things to see and do around the property. Firewood is available for purchase here. The whole family will have fun feeding the lambs, chooks and pigs, giving carrots to the friendly camels and donkeys, seeing some super cute chicks and grabbing some freshly laid eggs. The property has a spring fed waterhole which is a surprisingly lovely temperature for a swim. Don't miss the sunset down at Sunset Lookout or Little Mountain, and sunrise at camp is magic as the sun comes over the ranges. Get the fire going and enjoy a cuppa while you watch the show. There's excellent phone service here and a well-maintained road to get in.

Distance: 105km from Blue Range Warren Gorge via Hawker

Road type: Main road is bitumen but dirt road through the station

PARACHILNA GORGE

Parachilna Gorge is a quiet and large area with several free campgrounds within the gorge to choose from, some set amongst the cliffs of the gorge, along creek beds or on cliff tops. So take your pick but note there are no facilities.

A day trip to the historic North Blinman Hotel is a must for a hearty feed and a cold beer.

Distance: 86km from Mount Little Station

Road type: Bitumen

LEIGH CREEK

Leigh Creek is a great spot to grab some groceries at the Foodland, fill up with water, buy fuel and dump the toilet. The water point on WikiCamps wasn't suitable to pull a caravan up to, so we located a tap at the footy oval beside some BBQs.

Distance: 77km from Parachilna Gorge

Road type: Bitumen

FARINA CAMPING GROUNDS

Farina Camping Grounds has loads of history and is quite incredible, located at the old ruins of the Farina Township. Take a stroll through town to catch a glimpse of life many years ago.

This low-cost campground has shower and toilet facilities as well as amazing sunsets over the War Memorial. If you're lucky, you'll snag a spot with a patch of grass. Be sure to check out the bakery!

FARINA CAMPING GROUNDS

MARREE

Marree is a historic watering hole and railway town that lies at the junction of the Oodnadatta and Birdsville Tracks. In the 20th century the town was split in half, with Europeans occupying one side and Afghans and Dieri Aboriginal people living on the other.

Distance: 58km from Farina
Road type: Bitumen

COWARD SPRINGS

An outback oasis that was once a station on the old Ghan Railway. The campground is very shady and spacious, with designated sites. It is self-registration on entry into the campground and fees apply to visit the spa only or to stay overnight.

There are fire pits and quirky donkey showers, but the main attraction is the hot springs (though it's not really that hot!). This natural spa is open from April to the end of October and is a very small bore-fed spring. It makes for a very refreshing dip after a long day on the dusty roads.

Distance: 133km from Marree
Road type: Dirt

WILLIAM CREEK

Don't miss the William Creek Hotel, an iconic outback pub on the Oodnadatta Track, two hours east of Coober Pedy. With a campground, restaurant, pub and fuel facilities, it's well known for its scenic flights over Lake Eyre and the Painted Hills.

Distance: 74km from Coward Springs
Road type: Dirt

OODNADATTA TRACK SIGN

COOBER PEDY

Two hours from William Creek along a well-maintained track is the quirky and bizarre town called Coober Pedy, which has plenty of activities for the whole family. Make your first stop the iconic Coober Pedy sign with the massive truck and be sure to grab a picture here before you park up for the night.

We'd highly recommend staying underground! There is lots of underground accommodation to choose from, but we went with Di's Dugout (she has another place next door called Dinky Di's). It was sensational and can sleep up to nine people. What an experience and a lovely change from van life! The underground house offers all the comforts and facilities of a normal house with linen, cooking facilities, a laundry, shower and toilets.

If you're into opals and fossicking, there is a designated area open to the public where you can 'noodle' for opals. Head to the Information Centre and they'll mark the spot on the map for you, close to the corner of Umoona Rd and Old Water Tank Rd, near the outdoor cinema. The Coober Pedy Drive-in Theatre airs a movie every Saturday—check their website for film times.

When you leave Coober Pedy, be sure to stop in at The Breakaways for breathtaking views. It looks like Mars—it is where they filmed *Mad Max Beyond Thunderdome*.

Distance: 166km from William Creek

Road type: Well-maintained dirt track

☼ Tom's Working Opal Mine Tour, the Underground Bar (located in the Desert Cave hotel), Faye's Underground Home, Old Timers Mine & Museum, Umoona Opal Mine & Museum, Crocodile Harry's, Big Winch 360 (also great for sunset drinks at the bar), Serbian Orthodox Underground Church, Kangaroo Orphanage

🚐 BIG4 Stuart Range Outback Resort or Oasis Tourist Park

⛺ Coober Pedy Views

MARLA

Marla Traveller's Rest is a roadhouse, restaurant, campground, fuel station and supermarket about two and a half hours north of Coober Pedy. It has Telstra reception and is a fantastic spot to stretch the legs or pull up for the night. It has a pool too, with powered and unpowered sites available.

Distance: 235km from Coober Pedy

Road type: Bitumen

AGNES CREEK REST AREA

A free camp about 80km north of Marla that is well shaded and has loads of space. Enjoy an outback night under the stars and a drink around the campfire.

Distance: 86km from Marla

Road type: Bitumen

COOBER PEDY

NT BORDER SIGN

You can't cross the border and not get a picture! The kids (and adults) will also have a heap of fun on the border lines.

KULGERA ROADHOUSE

The first and last pub in the NT and the most central pub in Australia. It's an outback roadhouse with a massive can of XXXX gold and a couple of bogans (you'll know what I mean when you get there).

With a pub, fuel, restaurant, powered and unpowered sites, small playground and a mini mart, the Kulgera Roadhouse is a fabulous welcome to the NT.

Distance: 90km from Agnes Creek
Road type: Bitumen

ERLDUNDA ROADHOUSE

Erldunda is a remote roadhouse with emus, camels, powered and unpowered sites, a pool, fuel and spacious campsites. Check out 'The Centre of the Centre' (which puts you right at the centre of Australia!), the emu enclosure and the kangaroo farm as well as the sunset viewing platform. Stay in the unpowered section to save yourself some money and get the best sunset views. Even if you decide not to stay, it's a great stop to stretch the legs and let the kids see the animals.

Distance: 75km from Kulgera
Road type: Bitumen

CURTAIN SPRINGS

Curtain Springs is a remote cattle station providing accommodation for those travelling to and from Uluru. It also has a restaurant that does home-style meals, a store, fuel and powered and unpowered sites—unpowered is free of charge. It's a fantastic stop to use as a base to explore Uluru or as a stop on your way to Ayers Rock Campground.

Distance: 160km from Erldunda Roadhouse
Road type: Bitumen

Next stop Uluru!

See page 163 to continue the roadtrip north through the Northern Territory.

Eyre Peninsula

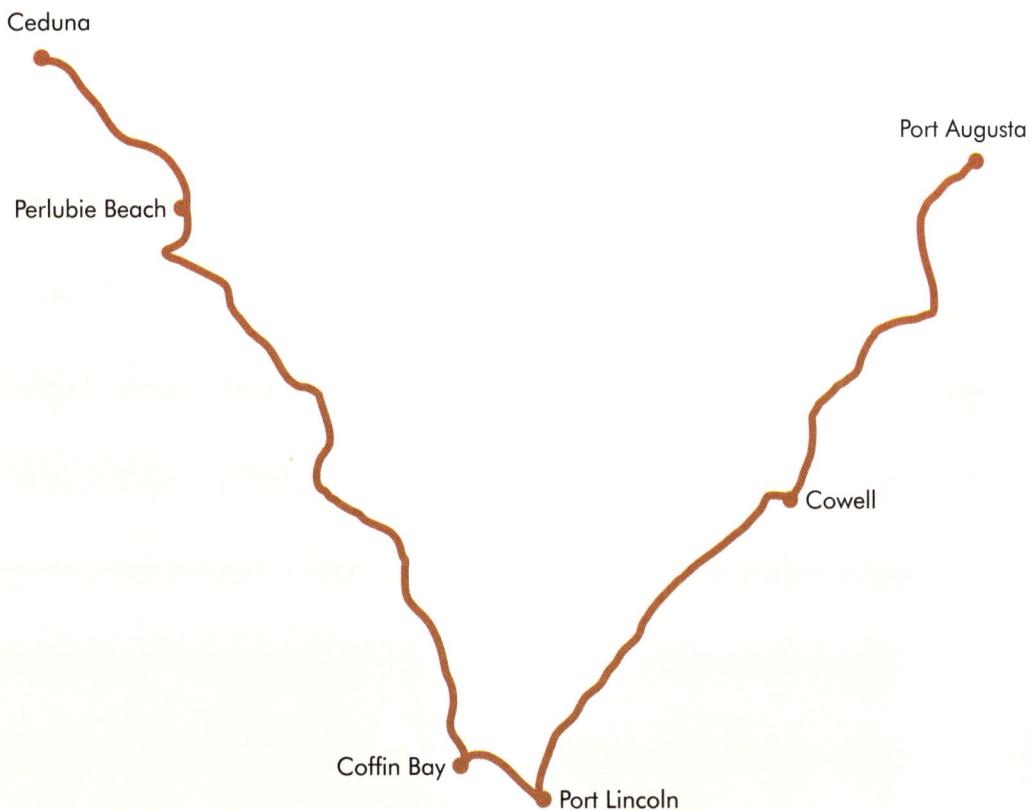

Ceduna

Port Augusta

Perlubie Beach

Cowell

Coffin Bay

Port Lincoln

PORT AUGUSTA

A growing tourism hotspot because of its proximity to the Flinders Ranges, the Eyre Peninsula and travellers heading to WA and the NT. The former seaport is now a road traffic and railway junction. If you need a supermarket, Port Augusta has a Woolworths and there's also an excellent skatepark for the kids, a Big W and other travel essential shops.

Distance: 308km from Adelaide

Road type: Bitumen

- ☼ Port Augusta esplanade, water tower lookout
- 🚐 Discovery Parks—Port Augusta
- ⛺ Port Augusta Sports Club Motorhome Park
- 🥤 Archer's Table

PORT AUGUSTA TO POINT LOWLY

About 80km south of Port Augusta is Point Lowly and if you go north from here, along a well-maintained dirt track, you'll find a cluster of amazing beach camps. They stretch along several bays and there are plenty to choose from.

Flintstone Beach at Point Lowly is absolute beachfront camping and is known for its dolphins. It's got magic ocean views and is a peaceful camping area. There are no facilities here but there is a dump point back in Point Lowly.

Distance: 89km from Port Augusta

Road type: Dirt track to all beach camps

- ⛺ Flintstone Beach, Point Lowly

WHYALLA

Whyalla is well known for its steel, beautiful coastline and friendly dolphins—and it's also the biggest spot in the region for retail shopping. An encounter with the dolphins is definitely not to be missed. All you need to do is visit the marina and wait for a boat to come in. They follow the boats right into the boat ramp and they sure do put on a show.

Distance: 35km from Point Lowly

Road type: Bitumen

- ☼ Point Lowly Lighthouse, Hummock Hill Lookout, Whyalla Foreshore, Whyalla dolphins, Whyalla Maritime Museum
- 🚐 Discovery Parks Whyalla Foreshore
- ⛺ Weeroona Bay Football Club, Knobbies Caravan and Camping Area

COWELL

Cowell is a fantastic regional beachside town that is currently going through a million-dollar foreshore upgrade. As you drive into Cowell, don't miss the famous silo art—it is vibrant and absolutely beautiful.

The foreshore is a welcome stop for families with a skatepark, a playground and a jumping pillow. If you're into local history the National Trust Folk Museum has a fabulous collection of memorabilia. The Franklin Harbour Hotel does a great pub feed and often puts on a pork spit roast (you may see it on the rotisserie outside the pub).

There's a dump point just out of town and a very friendly vibe here.

Distance: 106km from Whyalla

Road type: Bitumen

- ☼ Cowell Boardwalk, Cowell foreshore precinct, National Trust Folk Museum, Franklin Harbour Pub, swimming
- 🚐 Cowell Foreshore Caravan Park
- ⛺ Cowell RV Park

PORT GIBBON

CAPE HARDY

PORT GIBBON

Port Gibbon is a dune camp not to be missed. The ocean views amongst the dunes and opportunity to swim at your doorstep is incredible. If you take a stroll out to the point, you may spot a resident sea lion chilling on the beach.

Grab your boogie board and take a slide down the sand dunes. And you'll have the best seat in the house (within your van) for viewing the beautiful sunrises over the water.

There is a permit box on your way into the campground that takes cash and a dump point over at the Port Gibbon RV Park.

Distance: 22km from Cowell

Road type: Bitumen but the last 25km is well maintained dirt track

ARNO BAY

A very sleepy beach town, home to stunning beaches and an award-winning estuary mangrove boardwalk. The boardwalk is 1.4km with the reward of a beautiful lookout and beach to swim at.

The peaceful atmosphere of Arno Bay comes from the great community. Make sure you have a crack at some fishing—the area is known as the home of the kingfish.

The pub does a fantastic meal and has that remote feel with extremely friendly owners. A $20 note gets you three nights' accommodation out the back and a $10 voucher to spend at the IGA, at the local cafe or within the community's retail stores. A dump point is located behind the pub.

Distance: 28km from Port Gibbon

Road type: Bitumen

- ☀ Mangrove Boardwalk, Arno Bay Jetty, Arno Bay Foreshore, Arno Bay Pub, fishing, swimming.
- 🚐 Arno Bay Tourist Park—absolute beachfront
- ⛺ Arno Bay Pub

CAPE HARDY

This donation-only beachfront camp is one of our favourites. It offers ocean views, plenty of room and amazing sunrises, and it's only 20m from the beach for a surf. You're only a short drive from Port Lincoln now.

Distance: 50km from Arno Bay

Road type: Bitumen to the turnoff and then 6km of dirt road

TUMBY BAY

This gorgeous coastal area encompasses white sandy beaches, unspoilt coastline, blue waters and farming regions. Grab a bite at the Tumby Bay Bakery!

Distance: 38km from Cape Hardy

Road type: 6km dirt road and then bitumen

- ☀ Fishing, Tumby Bay Jetty, swimming
- 🚐 Tumby Bay Caravan Park
- ⛺ Lipson Cove Campground, Tumby Bay Self Contained RV Park

PORT LINCOLN

Port Lincoln on the lower Eyre Peninsula is a hub of activity and classed as the seafood capital of Australia. Allow some time for a sea lion tour and take a day trip to or camp at the Port Lincoln National Park. Take a swim at the jetty, visit the sculpture of famous racehorse Makybe Diva and enjoy a coffee or beer at the Pier Hotel overlooking Port Lincoln's waterfront.

Distance: 49km from Tumby Bay

Road type: Bitumen

- Sea lion tour (we can recommend Adventure Bay Charter), shark cage dive, Makybe Diva sculpture, Whalers Way, Port Lincoln National Park, Port Lincoln Jetty and swimming enclosure, Port Lincoln skatepark, Kmart
- Port Lincoln Tourist Park
- Bayview Park or Billy Light Boat Ramp Campground
- Boston Bean, Rogue and Rascal

LINCOLN NATIONAL PARK

This national park is incredible and the beaches here are untouched paradises. There are several campgrounds to choose from depending on your set-up and which way the wind is blowing. Do check the forecast before booking your camp as there is always a campground to escape the wind. Most of the campgrounds have facilities. Snorkel at September beach and make sure you keep your eyes peeled for seals.

Distance: 12km from Port Lincoln

Road type: Mix of bitumen and well-maintained dirt tracks

- Fisherman's Point (personal favourite), September Beach, Donington Beach Camp, Carcase Rock Campsite, Engine Point Campground—all suitable for a caravan

WHALERS WAY

If the weather is good, make sure you head out to Whalers Way. You're open to the elements here and if it is windy weather, you're in for a wild ride. This part of the Eyre Peninsula is an extraordinary stretch of coastline, and you have the option of day tripping or camping. Entry fees and camping fees apply.

There are several rockpools to explore in this area and I'd recommend downloading the WikiCamps app for their exact location. They are an adventure to get to but some of the best we've seen on our travels. Don't miss Whale Chaser Crevasse and Cape Carnot Lookout and blowhole.

Distance: 32km from Port Lincoln

Road type: Bitumen to the Fishery Bay Rd turnoff and dirt road from there

- Whalers Way (private land) or Redbanks

COFFIN BAY

Well known for its world-famous oysters, Coffin Bay is home to beautiful calm beaches, great fishing and a relaxed atmosphere. Take a drive down 4WD-accessible Long Beach with some lunch and a boogie board for the sand dunes and wait for the emus to stroll down the beach. They might even have a bath in the ocean for you.

If you are base camping in Coffin Bay, take a trip into the national park—wow! Seven Mile Beach is simply stunning, but if you're not keen on doing the trek out there, there are 4WD beaches you can park up on and swim at much closer within the national park.

If you love oysters try Coffin Bay Oyster HQ, which runs tours out to the oyster racks. Alternatively you can buy them at the takeaway shop next to the caravan park— they are as fresh and tasty as they come!

Distance: 73km from Whalers Way

Road type: Bitumen

Coffin Bay Caravan Park (the unpowered section is great)

Farm Beach or Big Yangie Bay

COFFIN BAY

FARM BEACH

A low-cost camp set on the absolutely picturesque Farm Beach. Facilities are available and if you're into fishing, this beach is most definitely worth fishing at. If you have a tinny, there is also a boat ramp.

Distance: 25km from Coffin Bay
Road type: Bitumen but the last 9km is dirt road

POINT DRUMMOND

Amazing views overlooking the ocean: a free beach camp at its finest. There's not much to do here but swim, surf, spot dolphins, relax and enjoy the sunset. A very picturesque campsite. Our pick is Point Drummond Camp 2.

Distance: 62km from Farm Beach
Road type: 10km of dirt road from the Flinders Highway turnoff

SHERINGA BEACH

A popular spot for sightseeing, surfing and fishing. A gorgeous beach camp where you can relax and take in the sunsets and coastal views. A permit is required to camp, payable onsite.

Distance: 55km from Point Drummond
Road type: 6km of dirt road from the Flinders Highway turnoff

ELLISTON

A beachside town in the alluring Waterloo Bay with a rugged and scenic coastline, a supermarket, a playground and a skatepark. Stop in for fishing, swimming, bushwalking and surfing.

Distance: 48km from Sheringa Beach
Road type: Bitumen

🚐 Waterloo Bay Tourist Park

⛺ Elliston Golf Club

☕ Sunnyside coffee van at Elliston Jetty

WALKERS ROCKS

A low-cost beach camp with a long stretch of white sandy beach. You can grab a campsite overlooking the beach or nab one further back in the campground, and there are toilet facilities available. Cracking sunsets and great fishing and snorkelling. Beach driving permitted and self-registration on site.

Distance: 14km from Elliston
Road type: Bitumen until the campsite

WOOLSHED CAVES CAMPGROUND

A rugged landscape with loads to explore. Talia Caves is only a short drive from this campsite—descend a set of stairs, take a left and walk into the ocean cave. If the water is calm, have a go at some crystal-clear snorkelling.

The rock pools in this area are some of our favourites and must be explored at low tide. Once you make your way down the stairs to Talia Cave, take a right and follow the rocks around the coastline—you can also check the rockpools out on your WikiCamps app. It is about a 10-minute walk and is well worth it, but take some shoes as the rocks are sharp.

Distance: 42km from Walkers Rocks

Road type: Bitumen until the campsite

MURPHY'S HAYSTACKS

A very unusual cluster of rock formations which will have the kids climbing and playing hide-and-seek. Read about Murphy's Haystacks at the information board and also contribute a gold coin before you walk in. There is some amazingly delicious honey for purchase. Either stop in for the day or stay the night at the campground.

Distance: 52km from Woolshed Caves

Road type: Bitumen

STREAKY BAY

Surrounded by some spectacular and unique coastal attractions, Streaky Bay with its charming atmosphere will have you relaxing by the tranquil waters and enjoying the township.

Distance: 41km from Murphy's Haystacks

Road type: Bitumen

- Shark replica, skatepark, foreshore swimming, jetty and swimming enclosure, The Granites and Cape Bauer
- Discovery Parks Streaky Bay Foreshore
- Streaky Bay RV Camping Site; Perlubie Beach (21km north)
- Bayfunktion Cafe

PERLUBIE BEACH

Most definitely one of our favourite beach camps in Australia. Absolute beachfront camping, and by that I mean you are parked up on the sand. Don't bother letting down your tyres as the sand is hard and easy to access. There is a toilet available and payment works on an honesty box system.

Phone and TV service, safe swimming for the kids, amazing sunsets and fantastic fishing are all available. If you have a tinny or are fishing from land at low tide, fish the weed line and drop your line into the sand holes for squid.

Distance: 19km from Streaky Bay

Road type: Bitumen

TALIA CAVE

TALIA CAVE

MURPHY'S HAYSTACKS

POINT BROWN/SMOKY BAY

A stunning coastline with ocean view camping spots—choose based on the wind and weather. Visit the beautiful rock holes and make sure you catch the sunsets because this is your last camp before the end of your Eyre Peninsula travels.

Distance: 53km from Perlubie Beach

Road type: Dirt track from the highway turnoff for approx. 25km

🚐 Smoky Bay Caravan Park

CEDUNA

Ceduna is busy with travellers because of its proximity to the Nullarbor. If you are crossing into WA, check quarantine laws for the food you are carrying before you stock up at Woolworths. Ceduna has everything you need and the foreshore is a lovely area.

Distance: 44km from Smoky Bay

Road type: Bitumen

☼ Head of the Bight, Ceduna Jetty, Ceduna Aboriginal Arts and Culture Centre, Cactus Beach, Penong and the Windmill Museum

🚐 Ceduna Foreshore Caravan Park or BIG4 Ceduna

PERLUBIE BEACH

PERLUBIE BEACH

THE NULLARBOR

The Nullarbor stretches across 1256km of flat desert plain through South Australia and Western Australia. Many think that it's a long boring drive and typically just punch out the kilometres as quickly as possible. But there is actually a lot to see and do on the Nullarbor. There's plenty of wildlife to see out your window, with camels, kangaroos and emus up close. Maybe you'd be interested in the longest golf course in the world, the Nullarbor Links? Stop in at the roadhouses that line the longest, flattest and straightest road in Australia or explore caves and sinkholes. You can even discover space junk that has fallen to earth!

PENONG

Stop in to check out the largest windmill in Australia at the Windmill Museum. Easy to pull a van up in front of it.

POINT SINCLAIR/CACTUS BEACH CAMPGROUND

If you love a surf, this campground has a really cool vibe and a wicked swell. Toilets, showers and fire pits available.

SCOTTS BEACH, FOWLERS BAY

Who would have thought you'd find a place like this along the Nullarbor? A fantastic paid beach camp overlooking the ocean, it is accessible only by 4WD caravan/camper trailer. You'll need to negotiate mud-flat tracks and a small sand hill to get in.

COORABIE FARM

Awesome stopover and welcoming atmosphere, with campfires, clean amenities and a beautiful farm setting. 8km off the Eyre Highway.

NULLARBOR ROADHOUSE

An excellent stop to stretch the legs and check out the murals, old roadhouse and iconic Nullarbor signs. Murrawijinie Cave, Koonalda Cave and limestone sinkholes are nearby. Don't miss the delicious burgers in the roadhouse restaurant.

BUNDA CLIFFS

The longest line of sea cliffs in the world stretches 200km, and they're absolutely spectacular. There's an easy dirt track in and you can free camp on top of the cliffs with magnificent views. It's not signposted so keep an eye on your WikiCamps app for directions. There's also a viewing platform further down the Nullarbor plain.

BORDER VILLAGE OR 10KM PEG BEACH VIEW CAMPSITES

Border Village is your last stop before crossing into Western Australia. It is here you will have a quarantine check so be sure you know the rules on produce—leave behind any fresh fruit, seeds, honey, and plant and soil material. The Border Village Roadhouse has a pool, and power and unpowered sites are available. There is also a restaurant.

The 10km Peg Beach View sites are completely free and give you stunning views over the ocean and magnificent sunsets. A dump point is available at Border Village.

The Nullarbor continues into Western Australia from here—go to page 121 to continue the journey.

Western Australia

Dampier Peninsula

Kununurra

Lake Argyle

Broome

James Price Point

Fitzroy
Crossing

Port Hedland

Karratha

Karijini
National Park

Bullara
Station Stay

Eucla

Perth

Hyden
Wave Rock

Lucky Bay
Campground

Albany

THE NULLARBOR

Once you pass Border Village in South Australia, the Nullarbor continues into Western Australia. There's plenty to see on this side of state lines too—starting with Eucla, just 12km along from the border.

Eucla

Eucla is an iconic part of the Nullarbor as it sits on top of an escarpment with ocean views. The ruins of an old telegraph station make a great photo and it's worth checking out the sand dunes, derelict jetty, caves and museum.

☼ Grab a pic at Border Village on the SA–WA border, Old Telegraph Station, Eucla Museum, Old Eucla Jetty

⛺ 10km Peg—beach view sites (beautiful views, Telstra service, sand dunes); 52 Peg camping area

🚐 Eucla Caravan Park or Border Village

Baxter Rest Area, Caiguna

This rest area has toilet facilities, dump point, bins and a picnic area, plus generators are allowed. It's a well frequented spot because of the sinkhole attraction close by.

Afghan Rock Rest Stop

This free camp is a great overnighter near the Balladonia Roadhouse, with Telstra reception, a natural pool (at times) and walking tracks to the actual Rock.

Fraser Range Caravan Park

A great outback experience. Friendly people, a communal campfire and great meals at the dining room. You may even spot a camel!

Membinup Beach

A national park beach camp halfway between Cape Arid National Park and Esperance. Zero facilities, but plenty of space and shelter. Absolutely free and surrounded by the most stunning beaches—our favourite is Wharton Beach.

Cape Le Grande National Park and Lucky Bay

One of the most famous beaches in Australia and a truly iconic place to see a kangaroo hopping along the beach, Lucky Bay Campground is a self-contained camp only metres from the beach, with toilets, showers and a camp kitchen.

- 4WD sand driving, Hellfire Bay, Frenchman Peak, Wharton Beach
- Lucky Bay Campground
- Lucky Bean Cafe

Esperance

Renowned for its immaculate beaches and natural beauty, this tourist town is slow paced with a friendly vibe.

- Cape Le Grand National Park, Stonehenge, Pink Lake
- RAC Esperance Holiday Park
- Esperance Overflow Campsite
- Downtown Espresso Bar

Hyden

A small town packed with natural attractions. Discover Wave Rock, a natural rock formation that is shaped like a tall ocean wave breaking, as well as Hippo's Yawn and Mulka's Cave. Take a dip in Lake Magic's saltwater pool or visit the wildlife park and pioneer museum.

- Wave Rock Caravan Park
- The Camp—Wave Rock Short Stay

Cape Riche Campground

A low-cost campground with toilets, cold showers and spectacular ocean views.

Albany

The breathtaking coastline of Albany is home to rugged cliffs, history and adventure. There is so much to see and do, and the view from the main street is spectacular!

- Two Peoples Bay, Historic Whaling Station, Little Beach, ANZAC Centre, The Gap and Natural Bridge, blowholes, whiskey distillery
- BIG4 Middleton Beach
- Bettys Beach

Denmark

This popular town is a hotspot for untouched beaches and towering forests. The rugged coastline offers unforgettable scenery.

☼ Elephant Rocks, Greens Pool, The Toffee Factory, wineries, Prawn Rock Canal

🚐 BIG4 Denmark Ocean Beach Holiday Park; Denmark Rivermouth Caravan Park (pet friendly)

⛺ Cosy Corner, Kronkup

Walpole

Walpole is well worth stopping in to take a wilderness walk above the treetops of the tingle trees, 400-year-old giants of the forest. Keep your eyes peeled for Grandma Tingle and the Giant Tingle Tree! A fantastic family experience.

Margaret River

Another amazing family friendly region in WA, with an array of activities for the whole family, everything from stunning farming country to beautiful beaches and fantastic breweries and wineries. Make sure you grab an attractions map from the info centre or caravan park in the region.

☼ Cape Leeuwin Lighthouse, Lake and Mammoth Caves, Farmers' Market, Colonial Brewery, Boranup Karri Forest, Country Life Farm, Prevally, Cheeky Monkey Brewing Co

🚐 Big Valley Campsite; Margaret River Tourist Park

⛺ Glenbrook Camping, Jarvis Estate Wines, Olive Hill Farm, Springwaters Estate

ROTTNEST ISLAND

THE PINNACLES

ROTTNEST ISLAND

Rottnest Island

An excellent day trip as you cannot take your caravan over there. The passenger ferry offers return family tickets, but keep an eye out for deals or vouchers online too.

☀ A meal at Hotel Rottnest, a selfie with a quokka, Segway tours, beaches and bays, snorkelling, SUPs, surfing. Lots to see and do—hire a bike!

Yallingup

Surrounded by national park and meaning 'place of love', Yallingup is a quaint beachside town which has bred some world-famous surfers.

☀ Yallingup Maze, Canal Rocks, Sugarloaf Rock, Dunsborough, Meelup Beach Road, Castle Rock, Geographe Bay, Swings and Roundabouts.

🚐 Yallingup Beach Holiday Park; Beachlands Holiday Park

⛺ Olive Hill Farm

Busselton

Busselton is one of the most family friendly locations with many beachfront features. The iconic Busselton Jetty is a stunning picture opportunity and we loved taking the train to the end of the 2km jetty.

☀ Busselton Jetty Train, Wonky Windmill Farm and Eco Park, Dunsborough, Meelup Beach, Cape Naturaliste Lighthouse, markets

🚐 Mandalay Holiday Resort; BIG4 Beachlands Holiday Park

⛺ Tuart Drive SC RV overnight parking; Busselton Farm Stay

Perth

To explore the city of Perth, base yourself at the awesome Karrinyup Waters Resort. It's central to everything and you'll be very comfortable here.

☀ Scarborough Beach, Cottesloe Beach, Kings Park, Fremantle Prison, Perth Zoo, Perth Mint, Aquarium of Western Australia, Fremantle, Scitech

🚐 Karrinyup Waters Resort

⛺ Yanchep Henry White Oval, Yanchep National Park

☕ The Daily Espresso

Cervantes

A small coastal fishing town and the gateway to the Nambung National Park, Cervantes is home to The Pinnacles, a desert area with ancient rock pillars.

☀ Lancelin Sand Dunes, sand dune 4WD, sand boarding, dune buggy hire, The Pinnacles

🚐 RAC Cervantes Holiday Park

⛺ Cervantes Oval

Jurien Bay

A popular tourist destination and only 25 minutes from The Pinnacles. 4WDing is very popular in the area, sea lions can be spotted at some beaches and there is fantastic squidding on the jetty. If you're stopping at The Pinnacles on your way through, there is caravan parking and you will need to unhook to drive through the national park.

☼ The Pinnacles and Cervantes, Green Head, Jurien Bay Jetty, 4WDing, swim with sea lions tour

🚐 Jurien Bay Tourist Park

⛺ Sandy Cape Recreation Park

Sandy Cape Recreation Park

Picturesque beach camping just north of Jurien Bay, and both 2WD and 4WD accessible. The main camping area has toilet facilities and a dump point and non-potable water. You need to be fully self-contained and camp fees apply. If you have an off-road caravan and take the dirt track at the end of the main camping area, Sandy Cove is great for more remote camping.

Cliff Head Rest Area

Awesome low-cost beach camping—pull up on the sand and enjoy the stunning sunsets overlooking the ocean. The campground is free and contains no facilities.

Geraldton

A great base from which to check out the premier wildflower location. The seaside town is a trendy city with art, coffee and plenty of shops. The town is home to beautiful inner-city beaches and an excellent foreshore precinct.

☼ Coalseam Conservation Park, Greenough Wildlife Park, Museum of Geraldton, HMAS Sydney II Memorial

🚐 Belair Gardens Caravan Park

⛺ 24-hour self contained RV stop; Coronation Beach Campground

☕ Quiet Life

Hutt Lagoon

Stop in to see the pink lake!

Lucky Bay Campground and Kalbarri

This resort town, based at the mouth of the Murchison River, is known for its stunning cliffs, beautiful beaches, wild pelicans and gorges.

☼ Nature's Window, Z bend, Chinaman's Beach, Rainbow Jungle, pelican feeding, gorges and sea cliffs, Port Gregory and Hutt Lagoon, Island Rock and Natural Bridge, Lucky Bay 4WD, beaches and sand dunes

🚐 Kalbarri Tudor Holiday Park

⛺ Galena Bridge; Lucky Bay Campground

☕ The Gorges Cafe

STEEP POINT
Mainland Australia's
most westerly point
26° 09' 5" S 113° 09' 18" E

SHELL BEACH

RED BLUFF

DIRK HARTOG ISLAND

Steep Point

Day trip there or ditch the van and take the swags overnight. Steep Point is an incredible place to visit with beautiful clear waters, great fishing and the westernmost point of Australia.

You can leave your caravan at Hamelin Outback Station Stay for a fee.

⛺ Shelter Bay on the sand dunes—pay the caretaker on the way in, permits required

Dirk Hartog Island

While you're out at Steep Point make a trip over to Dirk Hartog Island. The rugged and remote beach camps are truly incredible. Unreal fishing, sunsets, sand dunes and 4WD tracks. Take a look at our YouTube episode for more information.

Monkey Mia

Home to one of the world's best known wild dolphin encounters. An amazing experience, with pristine beaches and an excellent resort. Park day entry pass required.

☀ Dolphin interaction 7.45am–midday, yacht charter, boating, fishing, Denham township, Hamelin Pool, Shell Beach, snorkelling, Francois Peron National Park, Big Lagoon

🚐 RAC Monkey Mia Dolphin Resort; Denham Seaside Caravan Park

⛺ Eagle Bluff, Fowlers Camp, Big Lagoon Campground, Whalebone Bay

Wooramel River Retreat Roadhouse

On the banks of the Wooramel River. Relax in the naturally heated artesian bore baths, watch amazing sunsets by private campfires. Check the website for dinner availability. Showers and toilets plus powered and unpowered sites are available.

Carnarvon

A tropical destination and popular heritage area. A great place to grab supplies and for any car or van servicing and maintenance needed.

☀ Carnarvon Space and Technology Museum, Carnarvon blowholes, One Mile Jetty, Carnarvon foreshore

🚐 Coral Coast Tourist Park; Wintersun Caravan & Tourist Park

⛺ New Beach/Bush Bay Camping Area

Red Bluff

Located on Quobba Station, one of the most authentic, rugged and spectacular outback working stations. Renowned for its epic surf. It's pet friendly, with unpowered sites and drop toilets.

☀ Grab a meal and coffee at the cafe, take on the surf, Red Bluff lookout, stunning sunsets, fishing and snorkelling

Warroora Station/14 Mile Beach

A family-run cattle station on the coastline of the Ningaloo Reef, this is true wilderness camping where you'll step out of your camp onto white beaches and into warm blue waters. Self-sufficient camping, plus there's a dump point available.

☼ 4WD tracks, snorkelling, boating

Coral Bay

This gorgeous tourist town is protected from the Indian Ocean by the Ningaloo Reef. Perfect destination for sunshine and relaxation.

☼ Fishing charter, snorkelling, whale shark swim, glass bottom boat tours, quad bike tours, kayaking, stand-up paddleboarding

🚐 Bayview Coral Bay

⛺ Lyndon River Rest Area; 9 Mile Camp; Waroora Station

Ningaloo Station— Winderabandi Point

If you have an off-road van, you must come here! The beach camps are incredible—some camps are only metres from the water. Great fishing, snorkelling, sunsets and one of the best camps in Australia.

Cape Range National Park

Spectacular! From rocky gorges to the pristine waters of the Ningaloo Reef.

☼ Yardie Creek Gorge, Turquoise Bay, whale shark swim, oyster stacks snorkel, hiking trails

🚐 RAC Exmouth Cape Holiday Park; Yardie Homestead Caravan Park

⛺ Osprey Bay; Kurrajong; Yardie Creek

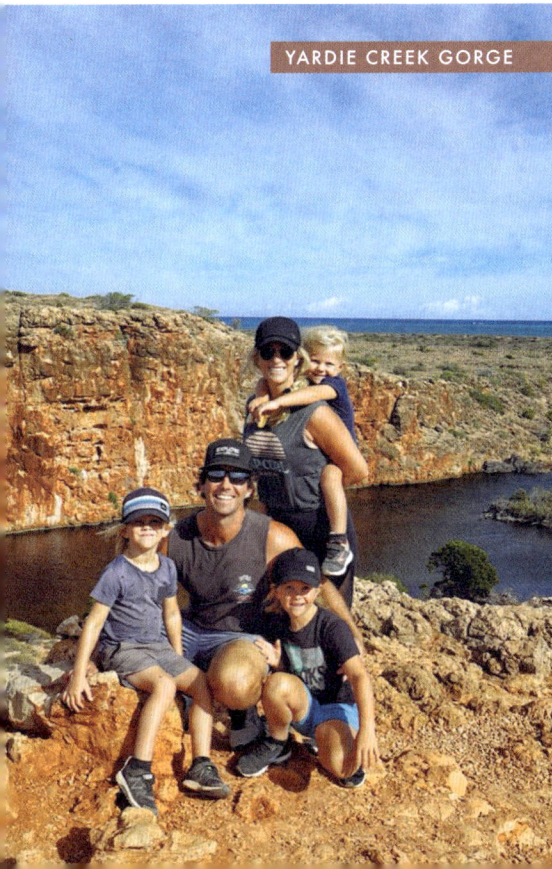
YARDIE CREEK GORGE

CAPE RANGE NATIONAL PARK

Exmouth

As the gateway to the Ningaloo Coast World Heritage Area, the tourist town of Exmouth boasts the 'Range to Reef' experience.

☼ Free spray park, Learmonth Jetty, Ningaloo Reef, Cape Range National Park, whale shark swim, Fig Tree Cave, Charles Knife Gorge, Bundegi Beach and boat ramp

🚐 RAC Exmouth Cape Holiday Park

⛺ Cape Range National Park

🥤 The Social Society

Bullara Station Stay

A working cattle station with the friendliest owners! Powered and unpowered sites available. They have damper and a campfire get-together nightly, or take in the sunsets at the 'Bull Bar'. Make sure you grab a coffee and warm scone from the cafe and please don't forget to have a tub in the outdoor woodfired showers at the station.

☼ Coral Bay, Ningaloo Reef, woodfired shower, kangaroos, coffee and scones

40-Mile Beach (Gnoorea Point)

Well known for being a fisherman's paradise, 40-Mile has private campsites overlooking the ocean. Fires permitted.

Karratha/ Burrup Peninsula

A pretty port town that contains massive exports such as iron and salt. Well worth a stop in for essentials (it has a Woolworths and a Kmart) but also to take some time to explore.

☼ Dampier Port, Cruise the Dampier Archipelago, Red Dog Memorial, skatepark, Burrup Peninsula, adventure playground

🚐 Dampier Caravan Park

⛺ Miaree Pool 24-hour Rest Stop; City of Karratha Overflow RV Site

Cleaverville Beach Camping

Great low-cost camping spot off the mouth of Cleaverville River—awesome fishing, a boat ramp and beach views.

Kialrah Pool

On the Jones River and slightly inland. A picture-perfect spot to free camp.

Tom Price

Situated in the Pilbara region, this mining town is on the edge of the Hamersley Range. The highest town in WA at 747m above sea level.

☼ Climb or drive Mount Nameless for sunset, tour the Rio Tinto iron ore mine, big mining truck, skatepark

🚐 Tom Price Tourist Park

⛺ R.I.P. Lookout; Tiger Eye Pool/Creek

☕ The Pickled Bean

BULLARA STATION STAY

BULLARA STATION STAY

KARRATHA

Karijini National Park

This tropical, semi-desert park is all about adventure. Amazing rock formations, plunging pools, stunning waterfalls and fantastic walking trails. You'll fall in love with this place.

- ☼ Hammerlsey Gorge, Circular Pool, Fern Pool, Hancock Gorge
- 🚐 Tom Price Tourist Park
- ⛺ Dales Campground; Albert Tognolini Rest Area

Albert Tognolini Rest Area

Free camping with amazing views and only a short drive from Karijini. Plenty of space to pull up and camp.

Port Hedland

The gateway to the Pilbara has a rich cultural heritage, Indigenous history and a Woolworths! It also has a fantastic skatepark, a swimming pool and more shopping if you need anything.

- ☼ Port Hedland Seafarers Centre Tours, Pretty Pool, Port Hedland Boulevard, Port Hedland Courthouse Gallery, sunset at the beach
- 🚐 Discovery Parks—Port Hedland
- ⛺ Port Hedland Golf Course; De Grey River Rest Area; Port Hedland Turf Club

Cape Keraudren

A fantastic beach camp within the nature reserve. A favourite for fishing, crabbing and remote relaxation. Toilets are available.

⛺ Dependent on weather condition, Sandy Beach or Top Camp (Boat Ramp)

Eighty Mile Beach/Anna Plains

Famous for fishing and shell collecting, this beautiful stretch of coastline offers stunning sunsets and relaxation. Powered and unpowered sites available.

☼ Fishing, 4WDing, shell collecting, swimming

Port Smith Lagoon

There is a caravan park situated here but nothing fancy. However, the lagoon is absolutely beautiful and a well-known swimming spot. Milky blue water, white sand and mangroves make for a stunning contrast. Good for fishing and swimmer crabs.

Barn Hill Station

On the breathtaking Kimberley coastline, this unique station is a great place to enjoy the sun and relax. The station offers powered and unpowered sites.

☼ Fishing, snorkelling, swimming, cave exploring, bush and cliff walking, rock pools

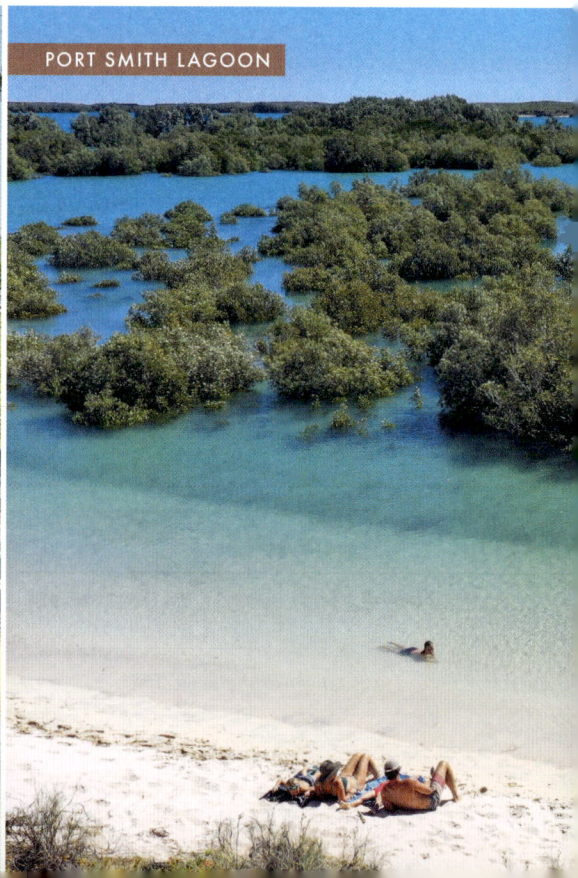

ANNA PLAINS

PORT SMITH LAGOON

Broome

A great coastal town with a fantastic atmosphere. The pearling and tourist town has plenty of attractions.

☼ 4WD Cable Beach, ride a camel at sunset on Cable Beach, Horizontal Falls, Gantheaume Point, dinosaur footprints, Malcolm Douglas Crocodile Farm, Roebuck Bay, Mangrove Hotel, Stairway to the Moon, Matso's Brewery

🚐 Cable Beach Caravan Park; RAC Cable Beach Holiday Park; Discovery Parks Broome

⛺ Willie Creek Free Camp, Quondong Point; Broome Pistol Club

☕ The Good Cartel

DAMPIER PENINSULA (4WD ACCESS ONLY)

Willie Creek

Known for its pearl farms, Willie Creek is also is a great free camp located on, you guessed it, the banks of Willie Creek. Good for sunsets, campfires and fishing. No facilities.

Barred Creek

One of the bluest creeks we have seen. Barred Creek is a bit of a tight track, but well worth it. You can camp at the bottom of the dunes or carry on further and camp out on the sand bank. Loads of turtles to see and fishing to be done. No facilities.

Quondong Point

A busy camp and for good reason. Easy access with plenty of spots to pull up at. Incredible sunsets and strangely you can swim and even spearfish here—the fishing is great too. No facilities.

James Price Point

Being in the landscape here actually feels like you're on Mars. It really is spectacular. Plenty of red dirt. Take a drive along the large red cliffs for a coastline you won't forget.

Pender Bay

A secluded campground overlooking Pender Bay with amazing sunsets and a relaxing vibe.

☼ Beach cave and rock pool, bathtub with a view, swimming and fishing, find the massive rock heart

Cape Leveque

A remote wilderness camp that's unique in its natural wonders.

- ☼ Cygnet Bay Pearl Farm, One Arm Point Hatchery
- 🚐 Cygnet Bay Pearl Farm; Goombaragin Eco Retreat
- ⛺ Middle Lagoon, Pender Bay

Mary Poole

A large free camp—depending on the season, there may be water. Plenty of room to pull up and have a campfire; it's a great stopover.

RAAF Boab Free Camp

A large area to camp and a great base to unhitch to visit Tunnel Creek and Windjana Gorge.

- ☼ Tunnel Creek, Windjana Gorge, Danguu Geikie Gorge, Mimbi Caves

Fitzroy Crossing

A stop in to break up the trip. The Lodge at Fitzroy Crossing is well-maintained, massive and green. The restaurant does some lovely meals. Do a day trip out to Windjana Gorge and Tunnel Creek. One of the highlights of our trip was walking through the water in Tunnel Creek. Make sure you don't forget your torch!

- ☼ Tunnel Creek, Windjana Gorge, Danguu Geikie Gorge, Mimbi Caves
- 🚐 The Lodge Fitzroy Crossing
- ⛺ Ellendale Rest Area; Ngumban Cliff Rest Area

CATHEDRAL GORGE

Bungle Bungles

There's both a caravan park and a free camp to stay at while you explore the Bungle Bungles. The free camp is awesome and it feels safe to leave your van there. You can only take a single axel caravan in—there is a campground within the national park. Check out Echidna Chasm and the beautiful Cathedral Gorge. An easy thirty minute walk gets you to the most breathtaking gorge.

☼ Scenic helicopter flight, Cathedral Gorge, Echinda Chasm

🚐 Bungle Bungle Caravan Park

⛺ Spring Creek Rest Area

Kununurra

A great base from which to explore the natural attractions of the Kimberley region, home to lakes, rivers, waterfalls and barramundi. There is more here than meets the eye.

☼ Molly Springs, The Hootchery Distillery, El Questro Station, Lake Argyle day trip, fishing the Ord River, Ivanhoe Crossing, Kelly's Knob

🚐 Kimberleyland Waterfront Holiday Park

⛺ Button's Crossing

🥤 Spilled the Beans at Kimberleyland Waterfront Caravan Park (not joking, it's the best)

KIMBERLEYLAND

IVANHOE CROSSING

Lake Argyle

This caravan park must have one of the most photographed pools in Australia. The park itself is a luscious and beautiful one. A Lake Argyle sunset cruise is an absolute must while staying here. Not only can you have sunset drinks while swimming in the lake, you'll also see rock wallabies and plenty of freshwater crocs, and there's a great cliff jump if you're game.

☼ Lake Argyle cruise, infinity pool, Argyle Homestead Museum, Lake Argyle Dam Wall

🚐 Lake Argyle Caravan Park

⛺ Maxwell Camp

Gibb River Road

Honeymoon Bay

Munurru King Edward
River Crossing Campsite

Drysdale River Station

El Questro Station

Manning Gorge

Derby

Tunnel Creek

EL QUESTRO STATION

EMMA GORGE

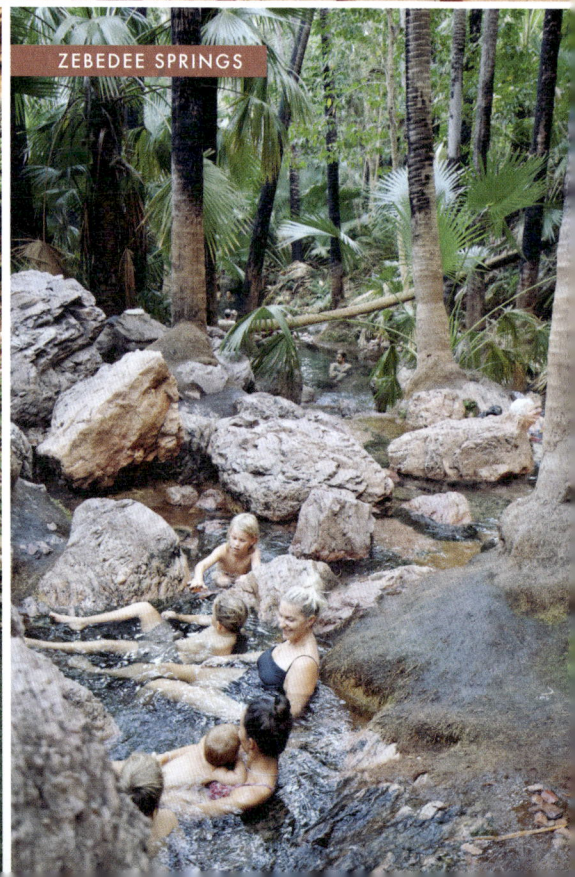
ZEBEDEE SPRINGS

THE GIBB RIVER ROAD

As Australia's most popular 4x4 track, the Gibb River Road is one big 660km epic adventure. As you turn off the bitumen and onto the dirt, the real journey begins. Driving over the range through the Kimberley is where it all starts and then it's on to majestic waterfalls, ancient gorges, swimming holes, untouched country and cattle stations the size of European countries!

We recommend allowing two weeks to really immerse yourself and properly see the Gibb River Road. If two weeks is too long, make a shortlist of the attractions you'd like to see for a quicker but no less exciting trip.

A wilderness permit is required to enter the area; it can purchased at Emma Gorge or El Questro Station reception.

EL QUESTRO STATION

Only one hour along The Gibb is the 1 million acre El Questro Station. It is a destination like no other and it really will blow your mind. Natural beauty is around every corner and there is a lot to see and do around the station.

☼ Emma Gorge is a 30-minute drive from the campground at El Questro Station. The walk into Emma Gorge is 3.5km, so allow an hour to get there. There are two swimming holes: Turquoise Pool and a waterfall and some thermal springs towards the right-hand side of the swimming hole.

☼ Branco lookout and/or Pigeonhole Lookout for sunset. Take a glass of champagne or a beer to toast away the sunset overlooking the mountain ranges of the station.

☼ Zebedee Springs is a permanent natural thermal spring that stays at a constant temperature of 28–32 degrees all year round. It is closed to the public in the afternoons to reduce environmental impact. This means the mornings are very busy so get there early!

☼ El Questro Gorge is not for the faint-hearted but it is probably one of the most incredible hikes we have done as a family. It is challenging, mostly shaded and cool, with plenty of swimming holes along the way. Allow five hours return.

⛺ The station has allotted powered sites, unpowered camping and private bush camping. The restaurant and bar are bustling with live music most nights. Unpowered sites open from 11am, no booking required, otherwise book the Black Cockatoo campground or a private campsite online before arriving.

HOME VALLEY STATION

Owned by the Indigenous Land and Sea Corporation on behalf of the Balanggarra Traditional Owners, Home Valley is located alongside the iconic Pentecost River and overlooks the Cockburn Ranges. This station houses an excellent resort-style pool, restaurant and bar, with grassy sites, a playground, tours and activities. Power and water facilities are available as well as showers, toilets and laundry.

We recommend getting on a fishing and hunting tour with Birchy. You can contact him through his Instagram page, @birchyfishingtourspty.

ELLENBRAE STATION

A million-acre property that is well known for its delicious scones, Ellenbrae is a cattle station that hosts an array of tourists throughout the dry season. If you do not wish to stay, stop in at the homestead, stretch the legs, grab a coffee or frappe and scone and let the kids play on the grassy play area.

Camping is not permitted at the homestead area but designated campgrounds are located nearby. There are donkey showers and some shady campsites.

GIBB RIVER ROAD CAMP

A free camping area located north of the junction of the Gibb River Road and Kalumburu Road, set on a creek bed with seasonal water. You can enjoy a swim, a rope swing and a fire at this shady camp.

DRYSDALE RIVER STATION

Sixty kilometres north of the Gibb River and Kalumburu junction, Drysdale River Station is a great stop with camping, fuel, tyre repairs, a licensed bar, meals and a small shop with some food supplies.

The station has powered and unpowered camping options with plenty of space to park up. Toilet and shower facilities are available. It is here you can grab yourself a Mitchell Falls permit or even do a scenic flight from the station over Mitchell Falls.

KING EDWARD CAMPGROUND (MUNURRU)

A fantastic campground to base yourself at while you visit Mitchell Falls. There is a very inviting swimming hole and waterfall at the campground where you can cool off from a day on the track. Fires are permitted and you can self-register when you arrive. There is also some incredible rock art to be found— ask about it at Drysdale River Station.

Depending on road conditions and traffic, the Mitchell Falls drive can take about two hours as the road can be heavily corrugated. If you are keen on a helicopter flight with HeliSpirit (we highly recommend it), do book prior to guarantee yourself a spot. There is no reception out there so you will need to organise this a few days beforehand.

☼ Mitchell Falls is one of the most iconic landmarks on the Gibb River Road with spectacular cascading falls. It is an easy walk to get up to the falls but a long 4.5km to the top. I promise, it's well worth the trek. We had booked a helicopter flight prior so we were down and back at the car within 15 minutes. Take your bathers and have lunch and a swim—swimming is permitted in the very top pool and near the helipad. Arm yourself with a hat and plenty of water as this hike is open to the elements with very little shade.

HONEYMOON BAY

Located in the far north Kimberley and on the coastline of the Timor Sea, this is an unmissable experience. Honeymoon Bay offers beachfront and ocean view camping, local guided tours, fishing charters, hot showers, flushing toilets, no phone reception but a free phone box and Wifi as well as a kiosk for snacks, bread and ice. You can also do washing here and launch your tinny off the beach. The closest town is Kalumburu which is 30km away.

The track has many washouts and is rocky and slow going—it takes about four hours from King Edward Campground.

Tip

If you're after some phone reception you're in luck at Gibb River Station. If you don't plan on staying here, there is a pull-over bay on the Gibb River Road, at the turnoff into the station.

HAAN RIVER

A free camp accessed on the south side of the Gibb. There are no facilities but it offers swimming in the freshwater creek.

GIBB RIVER ROAD CAMP

MITCHELL FALLS

DRIVE TO HONEYMOON BAY

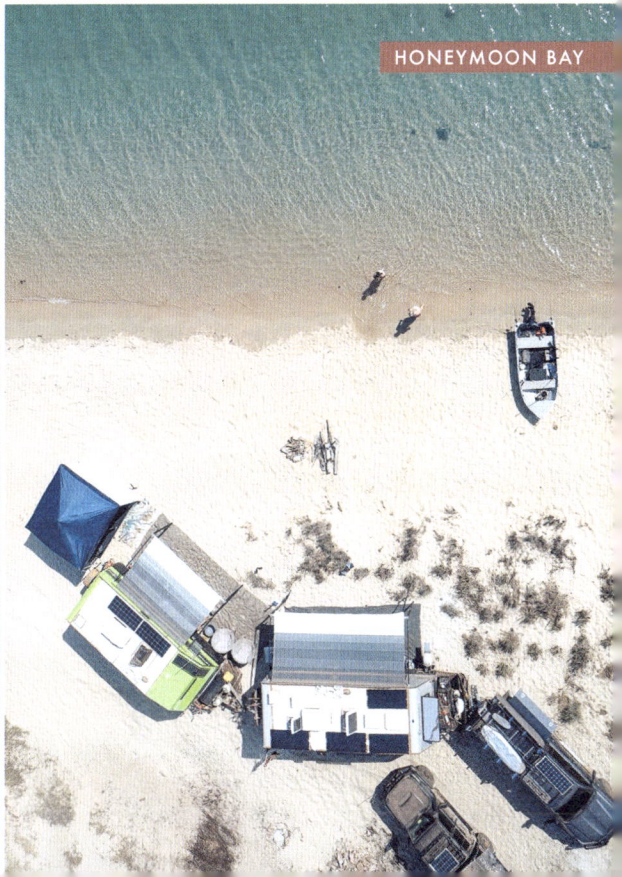
HONEYMOON BAY

MANNING GORGE

Mount Barnett Station, the halfway point of the Gibb River Road, is well known for its main attraction, Manning Gorge.

Take a look through the Mount Barnett Roadhouse as there is a great range of supplies on offer, including fresh produce!

Here you'll find directions on where to see the caretaker and pay your camping and day pass fees.

Camping is alongside the tranquil pools of the Manning River, about 7km from the roadhouse. There are amenities and there's loads of space but keep in mind it's a busy spot.

☼ Manning Gorge is about an hour hike (or 2 km) from the campground to the gorge and swimming hole. When you come to the Manning River, you'll have to swim across to begin your hike. Floating drums are available for you to throw your gear (or small children!) into for the short swim across. There is no shade on this walk, so aim to do it early in the morning, and take a hat and plenty of water. The Gorge is absolutely beautiful, with large cliffs and a waterfall. Finish off with a swim and rope swing back at the campground.

GALVANS GORGE

One of the most accessible gorges, only 1km off the road. This pretty horseshoe-shaped swimming hole and waterfall is reached via a very easy ten-minute walk alongside a creek. The kids will enjoy the rope swing and climbing tree.

ADCOCK GORGE

Accessed by a short 600m walk, Adcock Gorge is much quieter as it's less well-known. It is a deep green pool and has high cliff ledges to jump from. There is a lot of fun to be had here!

BELL GORGE—DALMANYI

Probably the most well-known gorge along the Gibb and part of the King Leopold Range Conservation Park. Since it's accessible from the western side and Derby, it is a very popular spot.

It is only a short walk until you reach the top of the waterfall, then you have to cross a rocky creek and get down a steep rock wall, which brings you to the bottom of the falls and the water's edge. There is plenty of space to bathe in the sun, go for a swim or have a picnic.

WINDJANA GORGE

A highly spiritual place with 300-metre-high cliff walls. There are a couple of trails to choose from but a simple stroll through the gorge at dusk is stunning. There are freshwater pools at the base of the gorge and you may just spot a freshwater crocodile.

An entry station is at the entrance to the national park and there is an unpowered campground with fire pits. Facilities are available but the campground is open for the dry season only. The road in is unsealed.

TUNNEL CREEK

A culturally significant site that was used as a hideout last century. The 750m underground tunnel is a great little adventure. Be prepared to get wet as you'll need to wade through some pools around knee deep, and don't forget your torches. The road in is unsealed and there are facilities but no camping.

DERBY

A small town located 220km north-east of Broome, Derby has a lot of interesting history and is known for having many boab trees. Don't forget to visit the Prison Boab Tree, a 1500-year-old tree that was used as an overnight lockup for prisoners. There's also a Woolworths in town.

TRIP IN A VAN
—

Northern Territory

Darwin

ARNHEM
LAND

Dundee Beach

Katherine

Timber
Creek

Victoria River
Roadhouse

Daly Waters

Barkly
Homestead
Roadhouse

Alice Springs

Uluru

—

Up the guts of Central Australia:

Uluru to Darwin

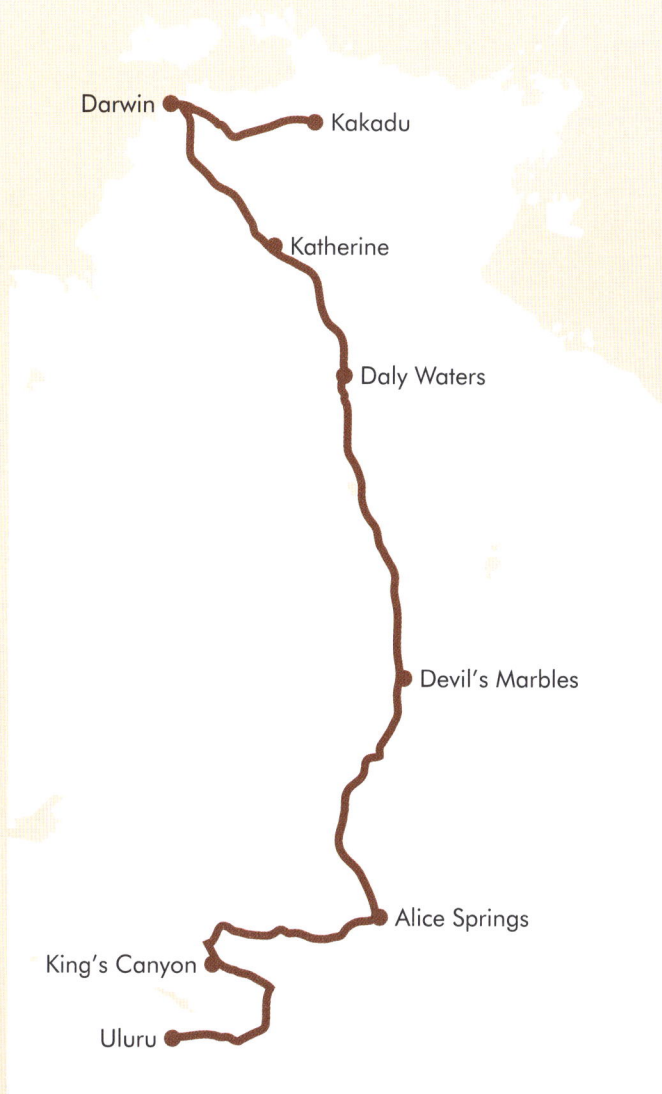

ULURU

Uluru isn't just a place, it's a feeling! Uluru for us seemed like 'just a rock', until we got there . . . It's a very special and beautiful place to experience.

We think sunset is the best time to be at Uluru. Park up at the sunset viewing area with some dinner, chairs and a few drinks and watch the sunset over Uluru in all its glory. You can even take a camel ride—we did so with Uluru Camel Tours. It takes about 1½ hours with nibbles and drinks provided afterwards. There is also a sunrise viewing area, which is a stunning spot to experience dawn at Uluru.

You must visit Kata Tjuta (a.k.a. the Olgas) and do the walk into Walpa Gorge. Even the drive towards the Olgas is really beautiful, and once you arrive it's an easy twenty minute walk right into the gorge. If you're lucky there will be some water at the bottom! We also recommend the Valley of Winds walk, and definitely check out the Field of Light, a fantasy garden spanning seven football fields.

Another fun way to see Uluru is by riding around it. It is a 6km track and you can hire bikes from Outback Cycles which are based at Uluru. You can also book their bikes online. We hired adult bikes and got a tag-along for Charli but we've previously hired baby seats for the adult bikes. You can use your own bikes if you have them, too.

There is a really great outback pub in Yulara that we stumbled across right beside the Camel Tours office. It's a great spot to enjoy a drink and it's also where they hold the Camel Cup.

We opted to stay at Ayers Rock Resort, a great caravan park with powered and unpowered sites, a pool, a playground and easy access to Uluru and surrounds. The dump point is a little out of town.

You can get groceries in Yulara at the IGA and there is phone service.

Distance: 107km from Curtain Springs
Road type: Bitumen

THE MEREENIE LOOP

If you have a 4WD, the Mereenie Loop is an adventurous and interesting way to experience the West MacDonnell Ranges. If you do the full loop (Uluru to Alice Springs via the West Macs, Palm Valley and Kings Canyon) you will cover 1330km of which 150km is dirt. Check the road conditions first as it can get very rough if it's not graded.

KINGS CANYON

Grab your hiking boots and explore Kings Canyon Rim Walk. Rising 270m above sea level, the canyon offers so much ancient beauty to explore with huge layers of sandstone, an oasis and natural rock pools. The Rim Walk is 6km, but don't let the stairs at the start deter you, they are the hardest part!

There are two options for accommodation: Kings Canyon Resort Campground and Kings Creek Station.

Distance: 324km from Uluru
Road type: Bitumen

PALM VALLEY

Coming from Kings Canyon, you can either make your way to Palm Valley or take a left and go towards Redbank Gorge. If you do go to Palm Valley, you'll need to backtrack towards the Redbank Gorge turnoff which is about 120km return.

Palm Valley Campground can be found down an easy track and is a fantastic national park campground with shady sites, flushing toilets, showers and communal fire pits. It's recommended that you drop off your caravan or camper before heading into Palm Valley as the track will require a 4WD. The loop walk and lookout walk are great hikes.

Distance: 224km from Kings Canyon
Road type: Only accessible via 4WD

KINGS CANYON

WALPA GORGE, THE OLGAS

ORMISTON GORGE

REDBANK GORGE

Sitting at the base of Mount Sonder, Redbank Gorge is a sacred site for Aboriginal people and a permanent waterhole. It is accessible via sealed road initially, with the last 5km into the gorge unsealed. There are several walks to do here, and the campground is well maintained with pit toilets, BBQs, fire pits and amazing sunrise and sunset views! Camping fees are payable onsite and are standard for all the Northern Territory national parks.

Distance: 118km from Palm Valley
Road type: Bitumen to 5km unsealed

ORMISTON GORGE

Who doesn't love a bit of sand in the outback to throw a beach towel down on? The gorge has a near-permanent waterhole, but it is mostly dry in the winter months (June–September). We were lucky enough to see it after a heap of rain when the gorge had lots of water. There are several walks you can do here: some 3–4 hour ones and other short tracks down through the gorge.

There's a campground and a little shop/cafe where you can grab a bite to eat and a coffee, as well as flushing toilets at the car park. National park camping fees apply.

Distance: 35.5km from Redbank Gorge
Road type: Bitumen

ORMISTON GORGE

ELLERY CREEK BIG HOLE

Ellery Creek is a popular spot for visitors to the West MacDonnell Ranges as it's perfect for a picnic and a swim but also for camping. It is recognised as a significant geological site and a permanent waterhole. Surrounded by tall red cliffs, you can understand why so many tourists flock here. You can hike the 3km Dolomite Walk and camping is permitted (NT national park fees apply) with toilets and BBQs provided.

On your way to Alice Springs, take a drive to Standley Chasm and do a self-guided walk. It is an 80-metre-high sandstone gorge which narrows to 3m in some spots. You can choose the short thirty-minute walk to the Chasm or longer trails. Accessible via sealed road.

Distance: 49km from Ormiston Gorge
Road type: Gravel road, suitable for 2WD

ALICE SPRINGS

Alice has absolutely everything and it's a good stopover for a week or more to unwind and top up on the things you may need (did someone say Kmart and Woolworths?). Alice Springs is well known for its beautiful desert landscapes and vibrant Aboriginal culture. There are often fun and quirky events on in town so make sure you head to the visitor information centre.

Check out the Kangaroo Sanctuary, the Reptile Centre and Alice Springs Desert Park. There's also the Museum of Central Australia and the Larapinta Trail.

We always choose to stay at the BIG4 MacDonnell Ranges. Though we don't love paying for caravan parks and usually prefer to free camp, we actually don't recommend doing that in Alice Springs. The BIG4 is an excellent park with loads to do for kids and adults: pancake morning, waterslide, BMX track, jumping pillow, pool, live music and a gym. See what deals they have going as they often have a good weekly rate.

Alternatively, you can daytrip in from Ooraminna Station Homestead, which is about 35km from Alice Springs.

Distance: 91km from Ellery Creek
Road type: Bitumen

DEVILS MARBLES

Karlu Karlu or the Devils Marbles is just over 400km north of Alice Springs and is a very popular conservation reserve that offers low-cost camping. Take a wander around these fascinating boulders that are strangely balanced and scattered across the valley. Toilets and open fire pits are provided.

Distance: 412km from Alice Springs
Road type: Bitumen

BANKA BANKA STATION

Located 290km south of the Daly Waters Pub and 100km north of Tennant Creek is the beautiful Banka Banka Station. Animals, memorabilia, a swimming hole, lookout, live music and a great atmosphere—and did I mention grass?! It's a lovely spot to park up and enjoy some tunes while the kids play garden games (large chess, bocce and Jenga).

Distance: 198km from Devils Marbles
Road type: Bitumen

DALY WATERS

Arguably the most iconic pub in all of Australia, Daly Waters without doubt deserves a stop in. There is so much history here—from murders and shoot-outs to drunken brawls—and they also think it's a little haunted. But don't let that stop you, because after a long day on the road, you'll want to stop in for a beer or wine and one of their classic pub feeds. The vibe and atmosphere are second to none, with live music every night, quirky things to see and an excellent campground. Plus, you can cool off in the pub's pool.

Get in early for a powered site, but there are unpowered sites available too. Fees apply.

Distance: 305km from Banka Banka
Road type: Bitumen

MATARANKA

Mataranka is renowned for its sandy bottomed thermal pools and there are two you must visit: Bitter Springs and Mataranka Thermal Pools. Take your GoPro or underwater camera and a pool noodle and float from one end to the other with the current.

The Mataranka Homestead is a lovely spot to camp and offers a bar and restaurant and caravan park facilities. Don't miss the Nathan 'Whippy' Griggs show at 8.30pm. He is a master at cracking whips and puts on a cracking (pun intended) show.

Little Roper Stock Camp is another fantastic campground that is ideal for kids! The owner puts on the most delicious johnny cakes and lets you hold his reptiles and feed his animals.

Distance: 168km from Daly Waters
Road type: Bitumen

☼ Mataranka Thermal Pools, Bitter Springs, whip cracking show at the Homestead

🚐 Little Roper Stock Camp, Mataranka Homestead

⛺ Little Roper Stock Camp

DALY WATERS PUB EST. 1930
UNATTENDED CHILDREN WILL BE GIVEN AN ENERGY DRINK AND TAUGHT TO SWEAR
ST WAYSIDE INN
BEEF 'N' BARRA
DALY WATERS PUB

KATHERINE

Katherine is a tourism mecca with plenty to see and do. Make sure you head to the Katherine Hot Springs five minutes from town for a warm and cosy dip, and do the Katherine Outback Experience with country music legend, Golden Guitar winner and horseman Tom Curtain, who puts on a show singing, breaking in horses and giving a working dog demonstration.

Cruise the majestic Katherine Gorge for spectacular views of the cliffs that line the ancient sandstone gorge.

Distance: 108km from Mataranka

Road type: Bitumen

☼ Katherine Hot Springs, Katherine Outback Experience, Katherine Gorge. Woolworths and Kmart if you're low on supplies.

🏕 Riverview Tourist Village

🥤 Black Russian Caravan Bar at the Visitor Information Centre (try the toasties too!)

EDITH FALLS

The picturesque Edith Falls are located in Nitmiluk National Park, 60km north of Katherine. You can enjoy a lovely swim at the base of the waterfalls and in the natural pool.

The pool is open most of the year, but it may be closed at times between November and April. Make sure you take your pool noodle. There are some fantastic hikes around the national park—we highly recommend taking the steep (but doable with kids) walk up to the Upper Pools. It's a 2km return trip and absolutely worth it for what we think is one of the best swimming holes around. Take a backpack, some water and lunch and I'll guarantee you'll have a brilliant time. There is a kiosk and campground at Edith Falls and plenty of grass to have a picnic on. The campground offers showers and toilets in a natural bush setting, with unpowered sites only and a 150m walk to the bottom pool. No generators and no pets allowed, but family rates are available. If you're unable to get a site (it's worth arriving early during busy periods) or don't want to stay the night, there are free camps about 20km back towards the highway.

Distance: 63km from Katherine
Road type: Bitumen

LITCHFIELD NATIONAL PARK

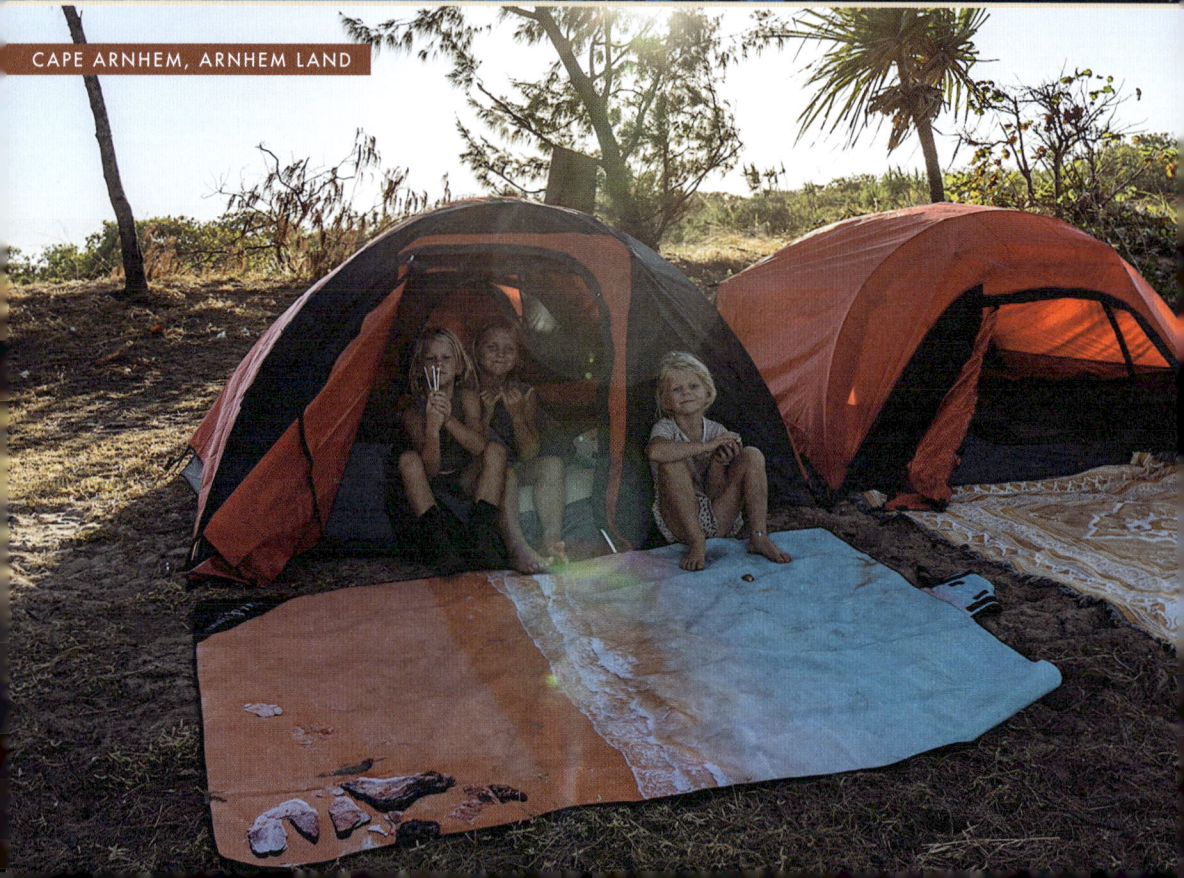

CAPE ARNHEM, ARNHEM LAND

PINE CREEK

Pine Creek has a lot of heritage and is a great stop to stretch the legs, grab a bite to eat or break up your driving days with a stopover. There is a fuel station and a public dump point if you're just passing through.

Distance: 68km from Edith Falls
Road type: Bitumen

- Lazy Lizard Caravan Park and Tavern
- Pussy Cat Flats Racecourse, Pine Creek (unpowered sites with a communal firepit and a bar to mingle at)

ADELAIDE RIVER

Adelaide River is a small but historic town on the Stuart Highway. There is plenty of WWII history here—check out the War Cemetery and Railway Heritage Precinct.

The Adelaide River Inn & Resort is a great accommodation option within the township as it has a bar and bistro, a pool and affordable rates. Choose Robin Falls Campground to free camp—it is spacious and the short walk to the three-tiered waterfall is simply beautiful.

Distance: 113km from Pine Creek
Road type: Bitumen

MOUNT BUNDY STATION

Located 3km from Adelaide River, this unique cattle station offers big grassy sites, a pool, an outback bar and delicious wood-fired pizzas. A great place to stop in and check out the heritage of the area.

LITCHFIELD NATIONAL PARK

Litchfield National Park is a must-see when you're in Australia's Top End. Think luscious waterfalls, relaxing rock pools and exciting plunge pools. You can either spend the day and see a lot or take it all in by spending a few days exploring.

To really experience Litchfield, we recommend camping at Florence Falls Campground or Wangi Falls Campground. National park fees apply and toilets and showers are available. If you'd prefer a powered site or caravan park, our go-to is Tumbling Waters Holiday Park, which boasts live entertainment, a licensed restaurant and outdoor movies.

Distance: 50km from Adelaide River
Road type: Bitumen (although some parts of Litchfield require a 4WD)

- If visiting for the day: Florence Falls, Buley Rockholes, Wangi Falls
- If exploring for a few days: The Lost City, Tjaynera Falls (a 3.4km walk), Tolmer Falls a.k.a Sandy Creek (a 1.6km loop walk), Walker Creek (3.6km walk and private swimming spots) and Surprise Creek Falls (4WD accessible only)
- Tumbling Waters Holiday Park, Litchfield Safari Camp
- Florence Falls Campground, Wangi Falls Campground

DUNDEE BEACH

A tropical oasis and relaxing escape, Dundee is one of the Top End's best kept secrets and a fisherman's paradise, with a restaurant, bar and pool, fantastic weather and a relaxed atmosphere! There is a boat ramp but also great fishing off the breakwall. Powered and unpowered sites available. Contact Justin if you're after some fishing spots via boat.

Distance: 160km from Litchfield NP
Road type: Bitumen

🚐 Dundee Beach Holiday Park

⛺ Dundee Forest Retreat

CRAB CLAW

Nestled on the water's edge for killer sunrises, Crab Claw is a great spot to catch a barra. There is a swimming pool, restaurant and bar, and it's just a fabulous place to relax and unwind. There's boat launching nearby and only powered sites available.

Distance: 50km from Dundee Beach
Road type: Mostly bitumen but the last few kilometres is dirt

BERRY SPRINGS

When making your way to Darwin, stop in for a lovely swim under the palms of Berry Springs. It's a very popular spot with a large picnic area, and the water temperature is absolutely perfect. Grab your pool noodles and float down to the larger pool areas.

CRAB CLAW BEACH

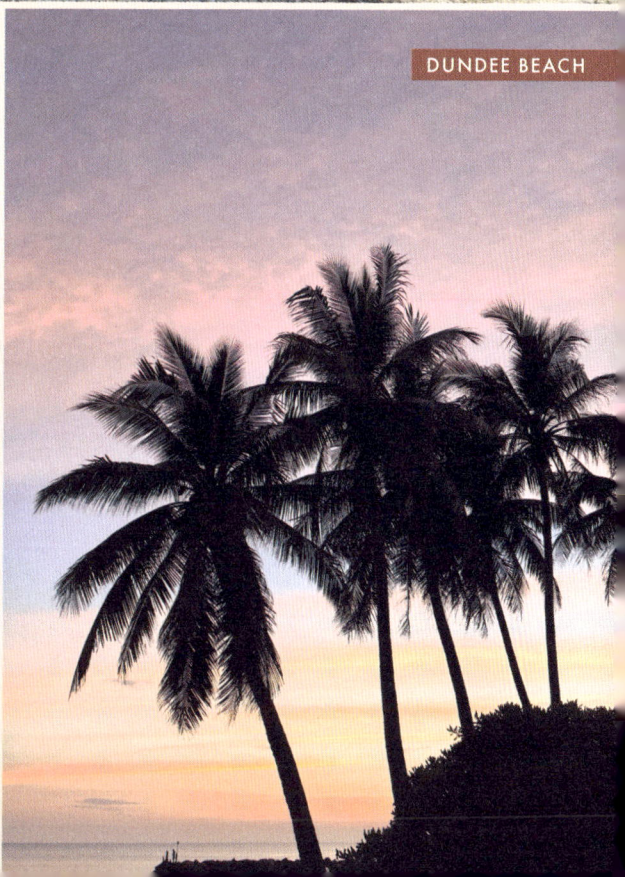

DARWIN

A fantastic family-friendly city with loads of attractions and free activities—we often spend about two weeks here. There is always something happening in Darwin, so check what's on online. It's an extremely kid-friendly city. If you're travelling without kids, note that Darwin's Mitchell Street has more pubs than any other street in Australia.

Distance: 118km from Crab Claw
Road type: Bitumen

☼ Mindil Beach Markets, Parap Markets (grab a famous laksa), Jumping Croc Cruise (we chose Adelaide River Cruises and they were fantastic), Darwin Waterfront Precinct and Darwin Wave Pool, Leanyer Recreational Park, Palmerston Water Park, Howard Springs Nature Reserve, WWII oil storage tunnels, Darwin Museum MAGNT (it's free and amazing), Crocosaurus Cove and Stokes Hill Wharf

🚐 Darwin Freespirit; Lee Point

⛺ Humpty Doo

☕ Postie on Bennett St, Darwin

KAKADU

Kakadu National Park is the largest park in Australia and is simply timeless. It is World Heritage listed and holds a lot of cultural significance. The landscape features stunning waterfalls, amazing rock art, Aboriginal artwork and wildlife.

Before entering the national park you will need a Parks Pass, which can be purchased online at the Parks Australia website and is valid for seven days. If you're unable to obtain this online, head into the visitor centre. A family pass is about $100 at dry season rates and adult passes are $40 each. There are low-cost camping and caravan parks available in Kakadu. All the caravan parks in the national park are brilliant so take your pick. There are several campgrounds to choose from depending on where exactly you are exploring.

Distance: 250km from Darwin to Jabiru
Road type: Bitumen

🚐 Cooinda Lodge

⛺ Jim Jim Billabong, Mardugal Two Campground, Merl Campground

☼ Ubirr Lookout for sunset, Cahills Crossing, Ubirr rock art, Jim Jim Falls, Twin Falls, Gunlom Falls, Yellow Water Billabong Cruises, Warradjan Aboriginal Cultural Centre, Maguk a.k.a Barramundi Gorge, scenic flights and Mamukala Wetlands

GUNLOM FALLS

GUNLOM FALLS

JUMPING CROC CRUISE

TO WESTERN AUSTRALIA FROM KAKADU

VICTORIA RIVER ROADHOUSE

A shady campsite with plenty of space, fuel, a restaurant, bar and amenities available. If you feel like stretching the legs, the Escarpment Hike is a great walk.

TIMBER CREEK

A great stopover and a shady oasis on an outback highway. You'll appreciate the pool and grass. Fuel and some groceries are available at this caravan park.

Timber Creek Hotel & Caravan Park

TO QUEENSLAND FROM KAKADU

BARKLY HOMESTEAD ROADHOUSE

This remote roadhouse is a welcome relief for outback travellers, offering a bar and restaurant, a shop, fuel, history, powered sites and a pool to cool off in too. Perfect for a stopover on your way to Queensland.

Top End Tips

- Take a sat phone, EPIRB or PLB

- Carry a first aid kit and snake bite kit

- Plan meals and stock up on groceries in places with large supermarkets (listed throughout)

- Communicate via your UHF radio and have it on while driving

- Drive to conditions and air-down tyre pressures

- Pack a map or have an off-road digital map such as HEMA explorer

- Tell your family or friends where you are headed if going out of mobile phone range

- Do not drive at dawn and dusk and aim to get to your destinations by 4pm. There are lots of cattle roaming and other wildlife such as kangaroos

- Take a spare tyre and a puncture repair kit

- Carry a spare air filter and a filter sock for your snorkel

East Arnhem Land

Banubanu Beach
Retreat

Gove Boat Club

Gove Peninsula Surf
Life Saving Club

Ganinyarra (Granite Islands)

Yirrkala Art Centre

Scout Camp
(Manaŋaymi)

Little Bondi
(Bariŋura)

Memorial Park Park (Gapuru)

ARNHEM LAND

Arnhem Land lies beside Kakadu National Park and the Gulf of Carpentaria and overlooks the Arafura Sea. It is in the far north-east corner of the Northern Territory and its wilderness area covers 97,000 square kilometres. It is rugged, beautiful, cultural and adventurous. Arnhem Land has two seasons: the dry season and the wet season. The dry season is between the months of May and September—we recommend visiting then. However, the locals tell us that the best months to visit are October and November, because of the unreal fishing and the lack of wind.

Permits

Arnhem Land requires a travellers permit which can be obtained from the National Land Council (NLC) website. You need to apply fourteen days prior to entering.

If you want to drink alcohol, an alcohol permit is also required and must be obtained via the NLC website or through the Permit Office, opposite the Aquatic Centre in Nhulunbuy. You won't be able to purchase alcohol in Nhulunbuy without both this permit and your ID.

Camping permits

Camping permits and bookings are required to camp in the Recreational Area campgrounds—this camping permit is called a Dhimurru permit. You cannot take your caravan to these campgrounds. If you are taking your caravan to Arnhem Land, you have only two places to camp: the Walkabout Hotel and Gove Boat Club.

If you are keen to trek out to the campgrounds, pack your tent or swag for a few nights and leave your van at the Boat Club or Walkabout Hotel.

Campgrounds

The campgrounds in the Recreational Area are wonderful. We recommend staying at Little Bondi, Macassan Beach, Turtle Beach, Cape Arnhem, Rainbow Cliff, Memorial Campground and Scout Camp. We checked them all out and they are very well maintained; you just need your permit to visit or camp.

Getting there

The distance from the Stuart Highway turnoff via the Central Arnhem Road to Nhulunbuy is 670km. There aren't a lot of places to camp along the way, so be prepared for a couple of big days of driving. The Central Arnhem Road is all dirt, and conditions vary depending on traffic and when it was last graded.

The Mainoru Store is located about 150km into the Central Arnhem Road. You can grab some fuel and camp out the back. It's spacious and very well maintained with plenty of grass and shade. Toilets, showers and power are available. Sometimes you can spot water buffalo swimming down the creek.

This is a paid campground, so please check the website for current fees: www.mainoruoutstationstore.com.au.

Flat Rock Creek Rest Area is set on a creek and is a free camp. It is a tight area, but you would fit a couple of vans in there.

Another unreal campsite is Jurassic Park Lookout, which isn't far off the Stuart Highway. With amazing panoramic views of the plain, it is simply beautiful at sunset. We recommend stopping in here on your way back down from Nhulunbuy.

Food and shops

You're in luck—there is a Woolworths in Nhulunbuy. The barge comes in on a Monday and they restock Monday afternoons and nights, so you're best to hit Woolies on Tuesday morning for fresh fruit and vegies, because come Sunday, they seem to be always low on stock.

The town has a chemist, post office, butcher, bakery, cafe, gym, doctor, physio, hardware store and bottle-o, plus a few other shops.

GOANNA LAGOON

A hidden oasis in the form of a freshwater lagoon with a narrow crevice to swim down. We had hours of fun here and you will too. It is covered under your Dhimurru permit to visit and is only about a twenty-minute drive from Nhulunbuy.

MEMORIAL PARK (GAPURU)

Wow factor. A stunning waterfall to sit beneath, plus little caves and a large waterhole (though we didn't swim in the waterhole as it didn't feel safe).

To get to this spot you need to book camping, even if you just want to visit. This is a sacred Indigenous area so there is a limit on people and cars. Only one camping site can be reserved at a time, so it is generally tough to get a booking, and you'll need to book well in advance. This campground is covered under the Dhimurru permit.

Latram River is a little further down the track and also well worth a visit.

SCOUT CAMP (MANAŊAYMI)

Not far from Memorial Park, and with the same requirements, is the much larger campground Scout Camp. Well maintained with fire pits, it's only a short stroll from the swimming hole. It has a set of rapids and is nice and shallow.

MEMORIAL PARK (GAPURU)

GANINYARRA (GRANITE ISLANDS)

GANINYARRA (GRANITE ISLANDS)

Located in the picturesque Melville Bay, Ganinyarra is only accessible by boat. If you don't have one, you can hire one through Gove Boat Hire. It is only a fifteen-minute trip from the Gove boat ramp. Your Dhimurru pass is required to access these islands. It is certainly worth the trip, with crystal clear waters and white sandy beaches. It's worth taking your swag (there is plenty of shade) and camping for the night as the sunsets are incredible.

BANUBANU BEACH RETREAT

On stunning Bremer Island is a slow-paced eco resort nestled in the coves of the Yolnu sea country. The retreat is approximately a fifteen-minute charter flight from Gove Airport or a one-hour boat transfer. Banubanu was built in partnership with the Traditional Owners to provide an island paradise for its guests.

Complimentary kayaks are available, and there are hiking trails and a wonderful restaurant and pool area—enjoy a cocktail while basking in the majestic views over the Arafura Sea.

If you are staying the night, there are beachfront bungalows on offer in one of the most remote locations in Australia. Catch a sunset at East Woody Beach. Take some wood, build a fire, enjoy dinner and take in the sunset views.

GOVE BOAT CLUB

LITTLE BONDI BEACH (BARIŊURA)

BUKU-LARRNGGAY MULKA (YIRRKALA ARTS CENTRE)

This centre is rich in history and boasts a large range of Indigenous artwork. Spend some time browsing the range and you may even be lucky enough to witness an artist creating a painting.

Just across the road is the Yolngu World War II Memorial Site, which is dedicated to the men who defended the shores of East Arnhem Land from Japanese attacks.

GOVE PENINSULA SURF LIFE SAVING CLUB

A licensed bar that also provides meals on a Friday night, its popular with the locals and boasts one of the best sunset views in Nhulunbuy. You can often see club volunteers patrolling the waters on weekends throughout the dry season.

GOVE BOAT CLUB

An excellent and atmospheric spot for a meal. It is popular on a Sunday night with locals and the playground and fig tree are a big hit with the kids.

Gove Boat Club campground is fully fenced and right on the beach, plus the hosts are great people! There are toilets, showers, a camp kitchen and laundry facilities available. We chose to stay here for the majority of our stay in East Arnhem Land.

LITTLE BONDI BEACH (BARINURA)

If you're not camping, we would highly recommend visiting Little Bondi. It is a spectacular local swimming spot with a good wave if you're keen on a surf, and the water is crystal clear. Little Bondi is covered by your Dhimurru permit and takes about an hour from Nhulunbuy—note it is 4WD only. The sand is a little soft so consider dropping your tyres. There is a drop toilet.

MACASSAN (GARANHAN) AND TURTLE BEACH (NUMUY)

Another scenic area to visit or camp. Macassan Beach is open to the elements but has the most beautiful rugged coastline. Do check winds before camping there, though! There are some rockpools and plenty of rope swings for the kids. Turtle Beach is yet another incredible hidden cove to visit in the area. You'll need a Dhimurru permit for both.

TRIP IN A VAN

Queensland

- Cape York
- Cape Tribulation
- Port Douglas
- Cairns
- Adele Grove
- Townsville
- Gregory
- Camooweal
- Airlie Beach
- Mackay
- Notch Point
- Yeppoon
- Hervey Bay
- Fraser Island
- Teewah Beach
- Brisbane
- Gold Coast

NORTH-WEST QUEENSLAND

Camooweal

The gateway to and from the Northern Territory. A spot to grab some groceries, explore and break up your journey.

- ☼ Camooweal Caves and sinkhole
- 🏨 Post Office Hotel Motel & Caravan Park
- ⛺ Camooweal Billabong

Adels Grove

A paradise situated in the Lawn Hill National Park. It really is a must-stop destination, and the beautiful water and remote location will blow your mind. It's got a restaurant, a fish and chips shack, a coffee spot and glamping tents.

- ☼ Lawn Hill Gorge, canoeing, Riversleigh Fossil Site D, Lawn Hill Cruise
- 🏨 Adels Grove, Boodjamulla, Lawn Hill National Park

Gregory

A small town located near the Gregory River. Grab yourself a coffee and a bite to eat at Billyhangers, which boasts 'the best coffee in the Gulf'.

- ☼ Historic Pub
- 🏨 Gregory Downs Hotel Caravan Park
- ⛺ Gregory River

THALA RESERVE

CAPE TRIBULATION

QUEENSLAND COAST

Cape Tribulation

Where the rainforest meets the reef.
A remote headland and coastal area of
the Daintree rainforest offering amazing
beaches, rainforest and scenery.

- ☼ Jungle surfing canopy tours, Daintree rainforest, Dubuji Boardwalk, Emmagen Swim Hole, Bloomfield River crossing, Bloomfield track, fishing
- 🚐 Cape Tribulation Camping
- ⛺ Cape Tribulation Camping
- ☕ Cape Tribulation Camping

Port Douglas

A blissful coastal town bustling with activity.
The perfect beachside getaway and a great
place to base yourself for the Great Barrier
Reef or just to relax.

- ☼ Butterfly Sanctuary, Flagstaff Hill lookout, Daintree rainforest, Palm Cove, Cape Tribulation, wildlife habitat, Rainforest Nature Park
- 🚐 BIG4 Glengarry Holiday Park, Tropic Breeze Caravan Park
- ⛺ Rifle Creek Rest Area
- ☕ Sparrow Coffee

Palm Cove

A tropical paradise, with balmy weather,
picturesque palm trees and beautiful
beaches.

- ☼ Jetty fishing, shopping, swimming
- 🚐 Palm Cove Holiday Park

DAINTREE RAINFOREST

FITZROY ISLAND

CRYSTAL CASCADES

BABINDA BOULDERS

Etty Bay

A hidden gem where the cassowaries roam free.

☀ Swimming, cassowaries, playground, fishing

🚐 Etty Bay Caravan Park

Mission Beach

A beautiful beachside town with plenty of holidaymakers. Keep your eyes peeled for a cassowary.

☀ Paronella Park, markets, Clump Mountain National Park, SUP

🚐 Bali Hai Beachfront Holiday Park; Beachcomber Coconut Holiday Park; Mission Beach Hideaway Holiday Park

⛺ Bingil Bay Campground; Hull Heads Recreation Area

Crystal Creek

A bush campground set in the Paluma Range National Park.

☀ Paradise Pool, Big Crystal Creek Rockslides, historic bridge

🚐 Big Crystal Creek Campground

Rollingstone

Overlooking Palm and Havana Islands, this is a relaxing beachfront location.

☀ Paluma and Crystal Creek rainforest, Paluma Range National Park, Balgal Beach

🚐 Tasman Holiday Parks, Rollingstone

⛺ Balgal Beach; Vincent 'Bushy' Parker Park

ETTY BAY

MISSION BEACH

Townsville

The largest urban city centre north of southeast Queensland. It offers plenty of experiences from the Great Barrier Reef to its beautiful esplanade and fantastic museum and aquarium.

☀ The Strand and Water Playground, Reef HQ, Castle Hill, trip to Magnetic Island

🚐 Rowes Bay Beachfront Holiday Park

⛺ Bluewater Park; Saunders Beach

Burdekin Cane Farm

A working sugar cane farm on Waterview Road in Brandon that isn't to be missed. As stated on the WikiCamps entry, 'Call prior to coming.' Large campsites, very affordable for a family and the chance to witness a sugar cane burn! The owners are very friendly, accommodating and knowledgeable. They also do cane farm tours. Powered and unpowered sites available.

Bowen

A charming town with beautiful beaches and the Big Mango.

☀ Horseshoe Bay, the Big Mango, Bowen Water Park Playground

🚐 BIG4 Bowen Beachfront Holiday Park

Airlie Beach

A vibrant tourist hub in the Whitsundays. Base yourself here for water and land activities.

☼ Whitsunday cruises, Airlie Beach Lagoon, Shute Harbour, Whitsunday Markets, Hydeaway Bay, Montes Reef Resort, day trip to Cape Gloucester and Dingo Beach

🚐 BIG4 Adventure Whitsunday Resort

⛺ Whitsunday Private Acres; Lake Proserpine—Peter Faust Dam

🥤 Bohemian Raw; Abell Point Marina; Fat Frog Beach Cafe

Hold It Flats

A tranquil farm stay and a beautiful property set on the banks of a running creek. Take your kayak or let the kids play on the rope swing. Campfires are permitted and only a short drive away is a scenic swimming hole and rope swing. Unpowered camping only.

Cape Hillsborough

A scenic coastline including rainforests, volcanic rock formations, beaches and rugged headlands. Renowned for its kangaroos on the beach!

☼ Sunrise on the beach with kangaroos and wallabies, Smalleys Beach, amazing walking trails

🚐 Cape Hillsborough Nature Tourist Park

⛺ Smalleys Beach

CAPE GLOUCESTER

CAPE HILLSBOROUGH

Eungella

A stunning countryside town, nestled in the hills of the Eungella National Park.

- ☼ Finch Hatton Gorge, Broken River to spot a platypus, waffles at Platypus Lodge Restaurant & Cafe, Araluen Cascades
- 🚐 Broken River Bush Camp
- ☕ Platypus Lodge Restaurant & Cafe

Mackay

You'll find whatever you need in Mackay, home of the Southern Great Barrier Reef.

- ☼ Bluewater Lagoon (free), aqua park, Sugar Shed
- 🚐 BIG4 Blacks Beach; BIG4 Mackay Marine Tourist Park; Andergrove Van Park (large unpowered section here)
- ⛺ Rowallan Park and Scout Club; Mycow Low-cost Camping Area

Notch Point

In our opinion, one of the best free camps along the Queensland coast. Off-road or 4WD access only. No facilities but a large grassy area to pull up to, plus palm trees, rope swings, fishing and beach views. Unpowered camping only and off-road caravans only. Otherwise take a swag/tent—it's well worth it.

Carmila Beach Free Camp

An unspoilt paradise with convenient beach view camping. Self-sufficient camping only. Toilets and dump point available.

- ☼ Fishing, 4WD tracks

Clairview BarraCrab

A caravan park with a fantastic view, beachfront bar, fishing, dugongs and both powered and unpowered camping.

- ☼ Fishing, spot a dugong, boating, playground
- 🚐 BarraCrab Caravan Park—its unpowered section is beachfront camping

Yeppoon

Gateway to the Capricorn Coast and Keppel Bay Islands, Yeppoon is a gorgeous family-friendly destination with beautiful beaches and 4WD tracks.

- ☼ Foreshore's Keppel Kraken Water Play, Appleton Park, Lagoon Precinct, Five Rocks 4WD track, Upper Stoney Creek, Byfield National Park
- 🚐 Beachside Caravan Park; Discovery Parks—Coolwaters Yeppoon (unpowered section is fantastic)
- ⛺ Junabel Farm Stay
- ☕ Lure Living

Agnes Water and 1770

A coastal tourist town which is situated at the start of the Southern Great Barrier Reef. A must-stop for relaxing, beachfront experiences and amazing sunsets at 1770.

☼ Paperbark Forest Boardwalk, Agnes Water Beach, 1770 Beach, 1770 LARC! tour, Lady Musgrave Island

🚐 Agnes Water Beach Holidays, 1170 Campgrounds

⛺ 1770 Southern Cross Travellers Retreat

☕ Agnes Cafe (just walk through caravan park)

Kinkuna Beach

Beach camping with plenty of shade and a gorgeous beach. A 4WD caravan is required because there's a sandy section as you get into the campground. It's a 4WD beach with hard sand and fishing to be done. Take a drive to Bargara.

Hervey Bay

One of the best places to see wildlife. With its calm waters, it's ideal for water sports all year round and a little paradise.

☼ Whale watching, the Pier, Wetslide Waterpark, Fraser Island

🚐 Scarness Beachfront Holiday Park

⛺ Maryborough Showgrounds, Fraser Coast RV Park

HERVEY BAY

HERVEY BAY

K'Gari (Fraser Island)

If you are looking for the ultimate camping and 4WD adventure then K'Gari has got to be on the top of your list. It's World Heritage listed and the lakes, beaches and rainforest are unforgettable. Keep an eye out for dingoes!

Inskip/Rainbow Beach

A very sought-after camp. Bookings online are required for this beachfront campground. Great fishing, incredible sunsets and only a short drive from Rainbow Beach for supplies. Self-sufficient camping.

Cobb & Co / Mothar Mountain Rock Pools

A family-run property that is well worth a stop in. Farm animals, freshwater billabong, playgrounds and a real nature experience. A coffee bar, a kids bike track and shower and toilet facilities will keep the whole family happy.

Teewah Beach

Camping on the sand dunes—does it get much better? Teewah is a nice hard beach so you can drive up at low tide and find a spot to camp. It's a short drive over to Double Island Point for great surf and another beautiful beach. Fees apply to camp at Cooloola Recreation Area.

Coolum Beach

A fantastic beachside town and laid-back lifestyle—what's not to love?

☼ BBQ boat Noosa River, Aqua Park Coolum, Mount Coolum

🚐 Coolum Beach Caravan Park

⛺ Noosa Sea Scouts, Noosa North Shore Campground

☕ Compound Secondhand Espresso

Stradbroke Island

Straddie is well worth the barge trip over, offering a fantastic beach camp and plenty to see and do.

☼ Amity Point, Brown Lake, Rufus King Seafood, North Gorge Walk, Cylinder Beach, Jumpinpin and sand dunes, Blue Lake, Adder Rock, Tripod Lookout

🚐 Amity Point

⛺ Flinders Beach Camping

☕ The Blue Room Cafe

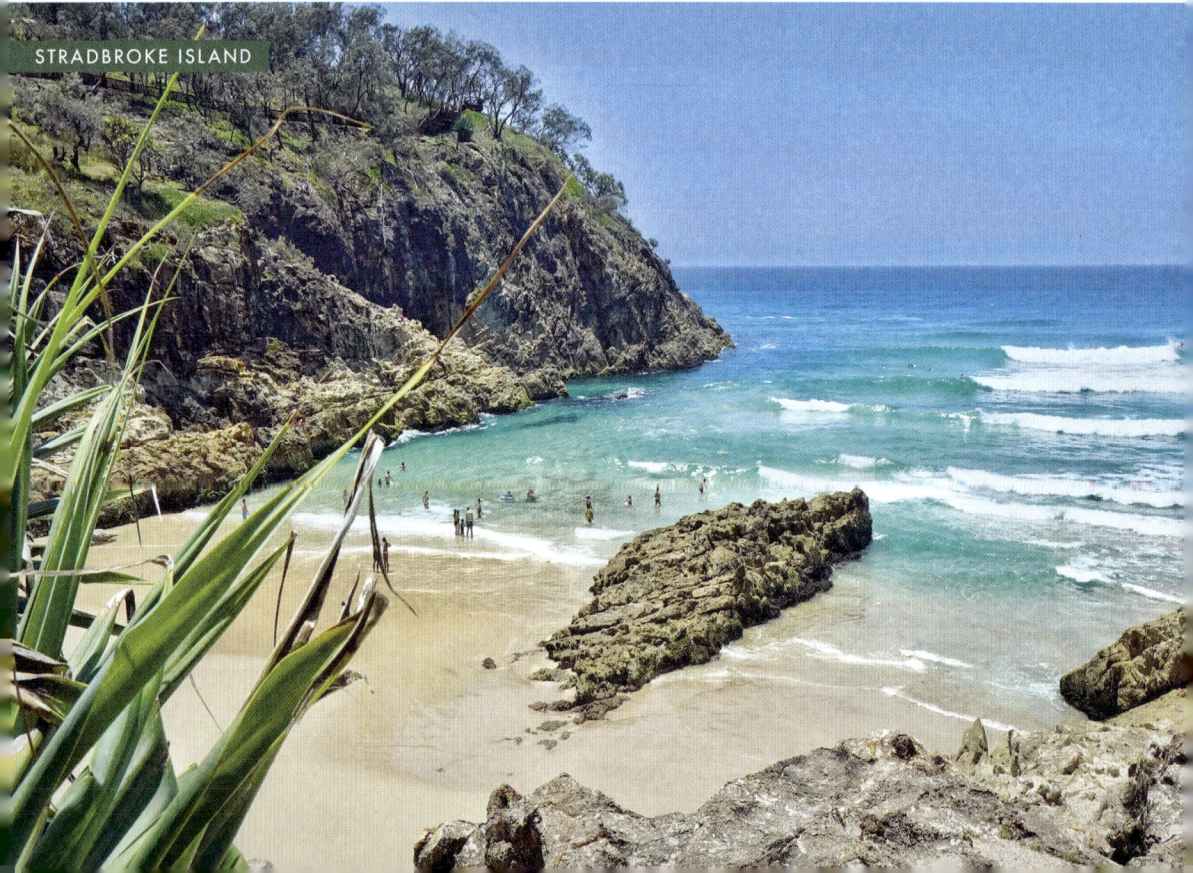

Gold Coast

The Goldie's long sandy beaches, great surf, amazing shopping and fabulous weather are what draw people from all over the world to visit! You need to try the Gold Coast at least once to experience it.

☼ Theme parks, Sky Point Observation Deck, Surfers Paradise, Currumbin Wildlife Sanctuary, Pacific Fair Shopping Centre, Burleigh Heads Lookout and National Park, Tallebudgera Creek

🚐 BIG4 Helensvale, Tallebudgera Creek Tourist Park, Burleigh Beach Tourist Park

⛺ Springbrook National Park

Curtis Island

A rugged island that's absolutely worth the trip. 4WD tracks, epic fishing, amazing beachfront camps and sunsets to die for.

☼ 4WDing, snorkelling, caves, fishing, swimming

⛺ Joey Lees Campground

CURTIS ISLAND

—

Savannah Way

(Lorella Springs, Northern Territory, to Cairns, Queensland)

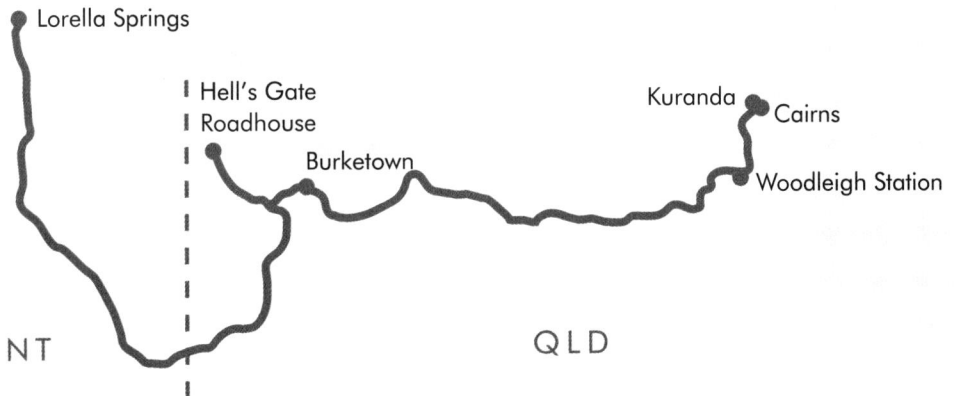

Lorella Springs

Hell's Gate
Roadhouse

Kuranda

Cairns

Burketown

Woodleigh Station

NT

QLD

LORELLA SPRINGS TO CAIRNS

The drive east out of the Northern Territory and into Queensland on the Savannah Way is an incredible outback experience. Get ready for loads of adventure, amazing sunsets and plenty of characters all the way along these dirt roads.

LORELLA SPRINGS

A million-acre, untouched wilderness sanctuary. Think waterfalls, swimming holes, hot springs, 4WD tracks and fishing spots. It really is an adventurous property.

It's best to visit Lorella Springs at the start of the dry season—around April or May when the waterfalls are flowing—as towards the end of the season (September) the water is beginning to dry up.

☼ Nanny's Retreat, Tristan Pool, Fossil Fern, The Waterslide, Alaska Pool, Nudie Hot Spring, Magical Hot Spring, Helicopter Pool, a secret fishing spot and Stockman's Swimming Hole

🚐 The Homestead—affordable camping fees apply and there is a restaurant and bar within walking distance of the campground. Small supplies can be purchased, but they're expensive.

Tip

Fill up on fuel and do a big shop in Katherine if you're coming from further west. However, by the time you reach this section of the Savannah Way you'll likely need to top up, and the best place to do that is Borroloola.

LIMMEN NATIONAL PARK

On the way out of Lorella Springs is the Limmen National Park—it's a deadset pearler. There are fire pits, spacious areas to pull up in, picnic tables, toilets and a beautiful sunset as always! The campground is superbly maintained and cheap as chips.

Pull on your runners or hiking boots—or thongs if you prefer—and take the easy walk around the Southern Lost City. It's full of amazingly unique rock formations with a lookout at the halfway point of the walk that gives you a great view of the landscape.

KING ASH BAY

Top End fishing heaven! The trek here is dirt road from Limmen until you hit National Highway 1, then 30km of bitumen to Borroloola, followed by 30km of dirt road, which is corrugated, but a grader does maintain this road at times so you may get lucky.

There is plenty of riverside camping at King Ash with powered sites available and great facilities like a bar and grill for happy hour, a boat ramp for those lucky enough to have a boat, and plenty of people around to have a beer with.

BORROLOOLA

The caravan park here at Borroloola has powered and unpowered sections, and Malandari Supermarket has groceries, but be prepared for some outrageous prices.

KING ASH BAY

LORELLA SPRINGS

SOUTHERN LOST CITY

LORELLA SPRINGS

HELLS GATE ROADHOUSE

From Borroloola via National Highway 1, across the border to Hells Gate Roadhouse, the road is unsealed and it's a 320km test of your corrugation endurance. The dirt road will hit you with some hardcore rough stuff—how rough depends on how recently it was graded. There are several free camps along the way.

Make sure you grab a picture at the border crossing into Queensland.

There is plenty of room to camp out the back and they also have a café, a bar with a happy hour and a night-time fire twirling show.

There is a good free camp called Hahn Creek Billabong 25km before the roadhouse.

BURKETOWN

From Hell's Gate Roadhouse there is a sealed road all the way to Burketown. Cruise in and hit up the bakery to grab yourself a coffee and delicious bakery goods.

- Albert River Free Camp (about 20 minutes out of Burketown). After driving through a small gate on the left, you will be on nothing but mud flats—drive another 8km to get to camp.

LEICHHARDT FALLS

A gorgeous free camp set on a clifftop overlooking the Leichhardt River. Chill here for the afternoon and soak up a campfire and yet another magical sunset. On the way, check out the Burke and Wills monument.

KARUMBA

A fishing destination and industrial port. Sensational sunsets and a sought-after spot to catch a barramundi.

- Waterpark and swimming pool, fishing, markets
- Karumba Point Holiday & Tourist Park; Kurumba Point Sunset Caravan Park

NORMANTON

Normanton is a great base for a few days. It can get very hot up this way, so consider staying at the caravan park. There are several mini marts and grocery stores here.

- The famous Normanton crocodile 'Krys', which is a replica of the largest crocodile ever in the world; the Purple Pub
- Get a permit from the information centre in town for limited riverside camping (but watch out for crocs!)

COBBOLD GORGE

Follow a 90km detour off the Savannah Way at Georgetown, with a maintained dirt track most of the way, and you'll hit Cobbold Gorge. Drop your tyre pressures all round to around 26psi. The road itself isn't that bad, but expect patches of heavy corrugation, dust holes, dips and a lot of loose rocks that pepper the front of your caravan—so drive to the conditions!

- Cobbold Gorge offers a short escarpment walk and a boat trip through the beautiful, narrow gorge (not recommended for kids under five); Ted Elliott mineral collection at Terrestrial
- Cobbold Gorge Caravan Park (infinity pool overlooking a dam as well as a restaurant and bar)
- Routh Creek Camp Site

WOODLEIGH STATION

GEORGETOWN

WOODLEIGH STATION

A large station property 326km from Cobbold Gorge with riverside and homestead camping available. There are flushing toilets and showers, a communal fire pit and the most epic sunsets. Lots of animals roam around free range and firewood can be purchased here. Plus, kids stay free of charge!

- Pinnarendi Station Stay Café (on the way to Georgetown)

LAKE TINNAROO

The lake is a popular tourist location for caravanning, camping, water skiing and, of course, fishing.

- Fishing, water skiing, boat hire, Lake Eacham, Curtain Fig Tree, waterfalls
- Lake Tinnaroo Holiday Park
- Barrabadeen Scout Camp; Genazzano Retreat Campgrounds

ATHERTON

A town located in the heart of the Atherton Tablelands. There's loads to explore beyond the town of Atherton.

- Wineries, historic village, Malanda Falls, Crystal Caves, Under Lava Tubes, Kuranda, hot air balloons at Ringers Rest
- BIG4 Atherton Woodlands Tourist Park
- Catch-a-Barra, Little Mulgrave; Ringers Rest, Mareeba
- Petals and Pinecones

KURANDA

Kuranda is a village in a rainforest and it is absolutely beautiful. Wander the shops, grab an ice cream, and visit the Butterfly Sanctuary and Rainforestation Nature Park. Drive or take the Skyrail for a unique perspective above the rainforest.

- The waterfall trail with Millaa Millaa Falls, Lake Eacham, Lake Barrine, Paronella Park, Herberton historic village, Crystal Caves, Curtain Fig Tree and Mamu Tropical Skywalk
- Lake Tinaroo Holiday Park—we suggest day-tripping from here
- Ringers Rest, Mareeba
- Coffee Works at Mareeba; Petals and Pinecones

CAIRNS

The bustling city of Cairns has a great atmosphere in a tropical setting. Geared toward tourism, it offers plenty to see and do!

- Great Barrier Reef tours, Daintree, Palm Cove, Crystal Cascades and Fairy Falls, Cairns Lagoon, Cairns Zoo
- BIG4 Ingenia Holidays Cairns Coconut
- Pride Gardens
- Tattooed Sailor Coffee Roasters

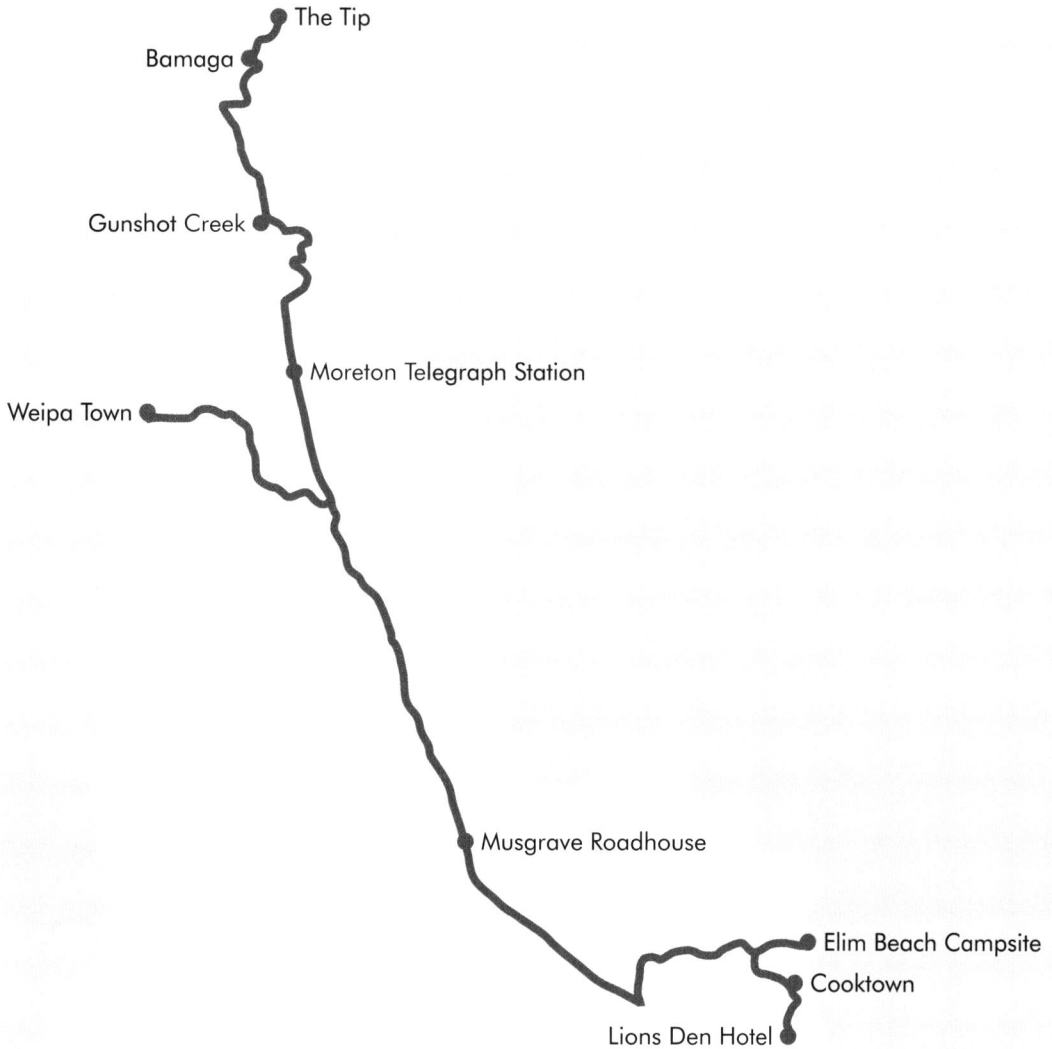

Cape York

The Tip

Bamaga

Gunshot Creek

Moreton Telegraph Station

Weipa Town

Musgrave Roadhouse

Elim Beach Campsite

Cooktown

Lions Den Hotel

CAPE YORK

When you're travelling Australia, Cape York should most definitely be on your bucket list. It's one of those locations that's bursting with adventure.

Timing your trip up to the Cape is imperative, as it can only be visited in the dry season from around April to November (depending on the rain). This is because of the tropical rain that descends on this narrow peninsula. The unspoilt wilderness is best explored outside of school holidays as campsites get very crowded. The Peninsula Development Road (PDR) and the Old Telegraph Track (OTT) are very busy with traffic towing trailers during this period.

There are several ways you can attempt Cape York. You could take your caravan the whole way via the PDR and skip the OTT. Or you could take your caravan, leave it at Bramwell Station Tourist Park, continue with your 4WD and do the OTT, then come back around and pick up your caravan to do the rest via the PDR. Or you could swag it, tent it or rooftop it the whole way!

We have done two of these options. We took tents and spent ten days travelling Cooktown to the Tip and back, and the next time we took our caravan the whole way via the PDR. We skipped the OTT, but we took the tracks off the PDR to visit Fruitbat Falls, Twin Falls and Elliott Falls. We took a portable chemical toilet along with our tent set-up, which came in extremely handy. We also packed a 12V shower—plug this into the car and out comes hot water!

Your Cape York route really does depend on your set-up and allocated time away. You may find you're not able to do it all in one go, but that just means you have to come back!

LIONS DEN HOTEL

Your trip to Cape York (in our opinion) starts here! A fantastic campground and swimming hole, and a pub with delicious pizzas to eat while you watch the kids play until dark at the playground. Loads of memorabilia and an iconic place to stop.

BLACK MOUNTAINS AND COOKTOWN

The Black Mountains are mounds of black rock that make it look like you're viewing a coal mine, but in fact they are lumps of dried-up lava, formed 250 million years ago. They are on the highway as you drive towards Cooktown, one of the most historically significant towns in Australia. Also check out Isabella Falls and Trevathan Falls nearby.

There is a great bloke in town who runs Nicko's Seafood—he does a seafood run every afternoon through the caravan park. Keep an eye out for him and make sure you grab some prawns.

After a couple of nights in Cooktown preparing for your trip, you have the option to put your van into storage and stock up on some last-minute groceries at the IGA; otherwise you're ready to hit the road.

- ☼ Grassy Hill, James Cook Museum, fishing, Finch Bay
- 🚐 Cooktown Holiday Park
- ⛺ Cooktown Racecourse
- 🥤 Driftwood Cafe

ELIM BEACH CAMPGROUND

Also known as Eddie's Camp, this campground is open all year round and is a perfect beach camp on your way up to the Tip. An absolutely magic spot with plenty of shade and unpowered camping. Be sure to check out the coloured sands while you're there and drive the beach at low tide.

WEIPA VIA THE BATTLECAMP ROAD

The well-maintained gravel road is a shortcut instead of driving back through Cooktown and Laura. It is here you will cross Isabella Falls—there is no bridge but the water is shallow. Stop in for a refreshing dip.

HANN CROSSING

There are several campsites to choose from. Pop into the ranger station to book an unpowered site. They are all waterfront and peaceful locations. Just don't swim—there are crocodiles in the lagoon.

MUSGRAVE ROADHOUSE

Great for filling up on fuel, grabbing a bite and taking a picture with the iconic sign. This roadhouse and station are heritage listed— it is the former telegraph station and was essential when communication in Cape York was first established.

THE LIONS DEN HOTEL

CAPE YORK

COEN

A small township to take a break. There is a public dump point here, a playground and a water fill point. Just a few kilometres north is a free camp on a freshwater creek. There are plenty of campsites to choose from. We chose to stay at the (Northern) Bend Campsite.

WEIPA

The road up to Weipa is generally pretty good as it is well-maintained with graders. It's a tightknit little township with just about everything you could need.

Weipa Caravan Park is a top spot to camp. With shady, grassy, large and some beachfront campsites, it's a lovely spot to stop and relax before the real adventure. The caravan park has a cafe on site called Barramunchies and there is a fantastic pool and a great atmosphere. Weipa is also where you will find the last big shopping centre as you head north. There is a Woolworths, tackle shops and a medical centre. As you head north there are still some areas where you can get supplies, but your next town for a shop is Bamaga. So look at stocking up at the Woolworths while you're in Weipa.

MORETON TELEGRAPH STATION

Located on the Wenlock River, 293km from the Tip, the station offers a spacious, shady, grassy and tranquil spot after a day driving. The campground has amenities and the shallow river out the back is a lovely spot to cool off.

BRAMWELL STATION AND ROADHOUSE

A cattle station four hours south of the Tip, Bramwell offers unpowered camping, fuel and facilities at the Tourist Park. Within the roadhouse you can grab a bite to eat as well as any essential supplies and merchandise. It is here that you can store your caravan before you go along the Old Telegraph Track. Turn left for the OTT or right to keep heading along the PDR.

OLD TELEGRAPH TRACK

The OTT is well known for adventure, camping off-grid and four-wheel driving. It is 82km long and it's slow going, but it can be done, on average, in a couple of days. There are several bypass tracks if you don't want to do the tough 4WD stuff but you still want access to the campsites.

The start of the track is pretty tame, with just a single vehicle track cutting through the bush with a few washouts and rocky sections along the way. Once you hit Palm Creek, the track starts to get a bit gnarly. A steep entry and exit into the creek make things a bit tricky. If you're towing a trailer, you will need to head to the right to find the chicken track or you will be winching up the exit.

BERTIE CREEK

A few more shallow water crossings, a couple of lumpy sections of track and you'll be ready to make camp. Bertie Creek is a fantastic place to make a stop and set up. A short detour off the track leads you to the point where the Bertie meets the Dulhunty, a quiet creek with rapids and crystal clear water. Set up camp, crack a few beers and jump straight into the cool shallow rapids.

GUNSHOT CREEK

After a peaceful night camping at Bertie Creek, continue north on the OTT. The next major landmark is Gunshot Creek and the notorious cliff drop that some attempt to drive through. For us, it was an easy choice to take the chicken track around—it leads you through the creek and up a steep uneven exit.

Gunshot is a good place to stop for a bit of lunch while you check out the track and watch a few others go through the creek. It can be very entertaining!

FRUIT BAT FALLS

Your next pit stop is Fruit Bat Falls, an iconic landmark of the OTT. You'll find the falls where the OTT crosses the PDR. A beautiful waterfall that cascades over a ledge into a shallow pool, it is perfect for swimming.

As you continue on the northern section of the OTT, you will soon come across Elliot Falls, another picturesque waterfall and pool that is probably our favourite in Cape York.

Only a few hundred metres away is the equally stunning Twin Falls. Tourists flock to Cape York to swim in these amazing waterfalls after an adventurous day on the tracks.

There is a national park campsite here if you book ahead.

SAM CREEK

Another brilliant swimming spot along the OTT, with free camping available. Logans Creek and Nolan's Brook are both excellent choices for a camping spot. Both are water crossings so make sure you have a snorkel on your vehicle.

At Jardine River Crossing, catch the ferry and cross the Jardine River. It is the only way to cross the river and you'll need to purchase a permit and ferry ticket. This can be done online or at the ferry terminal itself. The ferry crossing is quick—before you know it, you'll be north of the Jardine!

BAMAGA

Bamaga is the place to stock up and refuel. There is a bottle shop and an IGA. Be prepared to pay for expensive fuel and groceries here—remember you are in a very remote part of Australia! For a caravan park, stop in at the Seisia Caravan Park (powered and unpowered sites) and fish off the jetty.

Your other camping option is down the road at Alau Beach. There are powered and unpowered sites available, a pool, excellent fishing and beachfront camping, and you may even snag a hut. You'll find horses roaming the campground at times and you might spot a croc or two out the front of the camp. There's an unreal coffee spot in Alau Beach called Thupmal Coffee Espresso Bar.

Loyalty Beach is only forty-five minutes from the Tip and a beautiful beachfront campground. Powered and unpowered sites are available and it's covered in palm trees, with toilets and showers as well as a restaurant and bar. Plus, easy access to launch a tinny off the beach.

ROONGA POINT

What an epic spot Roonga Point is—beautiful blue waters and great fishing. We managed to catch a few fish and watch a stunning sunset. Plenty of room for campers and no facilities.

CROC TENT

The Croc Tent is full of Cape York merchandise, from stubby coolers and crocodile souvenirs to tanks and tees and croc tooth necklaces! Be sure to stop in for a look and grab yourself a map (only a few dollars) with the campgrounds and tracks on it.

Punsand Bay is a busy campground in peak season. There's always a great atmosphere, with hot showers, flushing toilets and a great vibe at the bar and restaurant. It offers a pool, powered and unpowered sites and beachfront camping.

YOU ARE STANDING AT
THE NORTHERNMOST POINT
OF THE AUSTRALIAN
CONTINENT

THE TIP OF AUSTRALIA—PAJINKA

You've made it to the Tip! Although it's not an overly difficult trek, it's still a lot of kilometres and a lot of corrugations to get here, so well done.

Park up at the bottom and walk over the rocky outcrop to get to the tip. It will take you about fifteen minutes. If you can get there on low tide, take a walk around the headland on the sand—it is a bit of a shortcut with magnificent views. Don't forget to take a picture with the sign and give yourself a pat on the back! Congrats, you're at the northernmost point of Australia.

THE WAY BACK

Once you have reached the Tip, the adventure isn't over just yet! Here's a few things to check out before you head back down.

Somerset Beach A great free camp.

Five Beaches Drive A scenic coastal loop that takes you past five beaches and back to the PDR.

Frenchmans Track Another challenging 4WD track that takes you to the east coast and Chilli Beach.

Chilli Beach A fantastic campground where the rainforest meets the snow-white sands of Chilli Beach lined with palm trees and with plenty of space to camp. You'll have a wonderful time here. Take a walk along the beach, do some fishing and have a campfire. There are drop toilet available and you can make a booking online. Pick your site and do your research as some do not have water views.

The Temple Located ten minutes from Chilli Beach. If you're keen to ditch the van for a different kind of experience, then this is your place. Jayson and Katie, who run The Temple, are some of the best people we've met and they do a great job running this WWII site that is off-grid living at its finest, with run-off water tanks and solar. It is a hidden gem in Cape York. If you're a fishing addict or dirt bike enthusiast or love a bit of history, The Temple has it all. An array of accommodation with built-in bunkers within the mountain, excellent food and good company will have you making the most amazing memories of this place in Portland Roads.

New South Wales

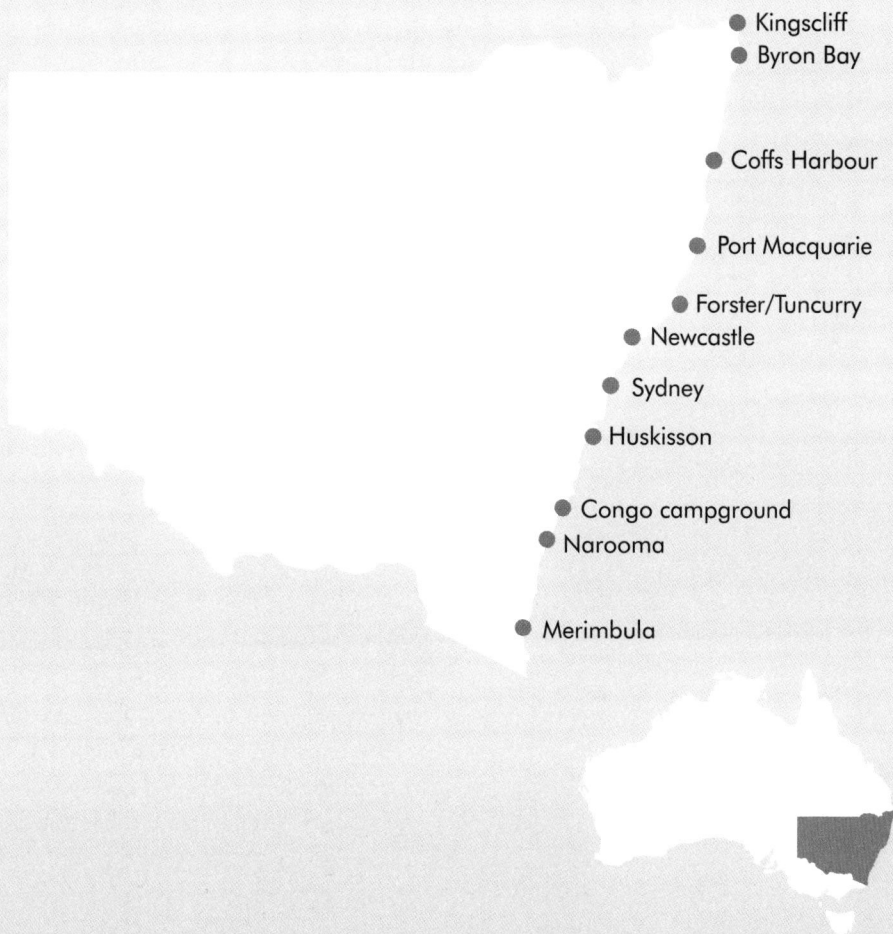

- Kingscliff
- Byron Bay

- Coffs Harbour

- Port Macquarie

- Forster/Tuncurry
- Newcastle

- Sydney

- Huskisson

- Congo campground
- Narooma

- Merimbula

Kingscliff

A popular beach holiday destination with gorgeous beaches, surfing and some fabulous place to dine or grab a coffee.

- ☼ Explore Pottsville and Casuarina
- 🚐 Kingscliff Beach Caravan Park
- ☕ Choux Box

Byron Bay

Byron has a great atmosphere in town and some lovely beaches. Although it's a very busy town, you've just got to stop in.

- ☼ Brunswick Heads, The Farm Byron Bay, Cape Byron Lighthouse and most easterly point, Wategos Beach, shopping, markets
- 🚐 BIG4 Byron Holiday Park, Reflections HP Clarkes Beach
- ⛺ Mullumbimby Showgrounds
- ☕ Top Shop

Evans Head

A popular holiday destination with great fishing and surfing. Nestled between two national parks, it offers plenty to do if you want a break from relaxing.

- ☼ Razorback Lookout, Broadwater National Park, Evans Head Living Museum, Chinaman's Beach
- 🚐 Reflections HP Evans Head
- ⛺ Black Rocks Camping Area

Red Cliff Campground

A national park campground; fees apply. Amazing views from your camp, beautiful sunrise and plenty of kangaroos roaming the campground.

- ☼ Yuraygir Coastal Walk, surfing

Illaroo Camping Area

Nestled in the dunes with views out to the ocean. Designated unpowered sites, fires permitted and great surf.

Wooli

A sleepy town located on the banks of the Wooli Wooli River. Delicious oysters, walking trails and great fishing.

- ☀ Yuraygir National Park walking trails, fishing
- 🚐 BIG4 Solitary Islands Resort
- ⛺ Boorkoom Campground

Pebbly Beach Campground

Amazing beach campsites and only 4WD accessible. There's beach driving to get to the campground and you must cross Station Creek at low tide to access the campground. National park fees apply.

- ☀ Station Creek Campground swimming spot; Station Creek on Pebbly Beach side

Coffs Harbour

Famous for the Big Banana, this beautiful seaside city has plenty of attractions. From the Solitary Islands Marine Park to butterflies and beaches, you won't run out of things to do.

- ☀ Big Banana Fun Park, aquarium, Butterfly House, Muttonbird Island Walk, trip to Moonee Beach
- 🚐 Big4 Park Beach Holiday Park
- ⛺ Coffs Leagues Club

Nambucca Heads

A gorgeous coastal holiday town with majestic beaches and inlets—you can swim as well as taking in the view from several amazing lookouts.

- ☀ V-Wall, Nambucca River cruise, Captain Cook's Lookout
- 🚐 Ingenia Holidays White Albatross
- ⛺ Lions Park—Macksville; Gumma Reserve, Nambucca Bowling Club

Scotts Head

A lovely coastal village and a relaxing place to visit. Excellent surfing and dog friendly.

- ☀ Beaches, surfing
- 🚐 Reflections Holiday Park Scotts Head
- ⛺ Gumma Reserve

South West Rocks

The perfect escape for a beachside family trip, enriched with heritage and stunning landscapes.

- ☼ Lighthouse (the tallest), Trial Bay Gaol, bushwalking, diving, wildlife
- 🚐 Horseshoe Bay Holiday Park
- ⛺ Trial Bay Gaol

Crescent Head

This coastal town overlooks one of the most renowned righthand surf breaks. A fantastic beach, so try to get a beachfront site if you can!

- ☼ SUP, surfing, fishing, Hat Head National Park, Slim Dusty Centre
- 🚐 Crescent Head Holiday Park
- ⛺ Delicate Nobby, Point Plomer Campground
- ☕ Blackfish Coffee

Point Plomer

A fabulous low-cost self-sufficient camp. Plenty of grassy areas with beach views and safe swimming for the kids. A great wave too. Toilets and cold showers.

Waves Campground just down the road

Port Macquarie

A beautiful coastal destination nestled in between the ocean and the river.

- ☼ Koala Hospital, colourful rocks on Port Macquarie breakwall, Flynn's Beach, Town Beach, Ricardoes Tomatoes, Lighthouse and Lighthouse Beach
- 🚐 NRMA Port Macquarie Breakwall Holiday Park
- ⛺ Point Plomer Campground; Wauchope Showgrounds
- ☕ Group Therapy Coffee

Forster/Tuncurry

These twin towns were built where the lake meets the ocean. Surrounded by national parks and secluded beaches, Forster Tuncurry has some mind-blowing headlands.

- ☼ Booti Booti National Park, Cape Hawke Lookout, Bennetts Head Lookout, Myall Lakes at Neranie Campground, Boomerang Beach, Blueys Beach
- 🚐 BIG4 Great Lakes at Forster Tuncurry; Reflections HP Forster
- ⛺ The Ruins Campground, Booti Booti National Park; Neranie Campground, Myall Lakes

Seal Rocks

This little holiday village is a gorgeous pocket of paradise. Known for its unspoiled surf and an impressive lighthouse, it offers a sense of isolation that will have you very relaxed.

- ☼ Sugarloaf Point Lighthouse, diving, surfing, SUP
- 🚐 Reflections HP Seal Rocks
- ⛺ Treachery Camp
- ☕ Treachery Camp Coffee Van

Port Stephens

A relaxing yet adventurous coastal area with beautiful beaches and bays. Wineries, breweries, sand dunes, dolphin and whale watching—there's plenty for everyone to enjoy!

- ☼ 4WD sand-duning, quad bike dune tours, Mount Tomaree Lookout, Oakvale Farm, Toboggan Hill Park
- 🚐 Fingal Bay Holiday Park; Halifax Holiday Park; Shoal Bay Holiday Park
- ⛺ Samurai Beach Camping Ground (4WD + off-road caravan required)

Newcastle

A breathtaking coastline with plenty of beaches, ocean baths and a hub of activity.

- ☼ Stockton Dunes, Fort Scratchley, Caves Beach cave, Bogey Hole, King Edward Park, Nobby Head Lookout, Hunter Valley wineries, Hunter Valley Gardens, Blackbutt Reserve
- 🚐 Swansea Gardens Holiday Park; Stockton Beach Holiday Park
- ⛺ Morisset Showground; Maitland Showground; Kurri Kurri Sports Ground
- ☕ Blue Door Kiosk, Mereweather Beach

Toowoon Bay

Nestled on a headland between two beautiful beaches, with protected bays for swimming.

- ☼ Pelican feeding, heritage walk, Wyong Milk Factory, Norah Head Lighthouse, Amazement Farm & Fun Park
- 🚐 Toowoon Bay Holiday Park
- ⛺ Freemans Campground Lake Munmorah (book on national park website)

Sydney

If you haven't been to Sydney, visiting Sydney Harbour and the Opera House on your lap of Australia is a must. There are plenty of attractions and the public transport is sensational.

- ☼ Bondi Beach, Sydney Opera House, Harbour Bridge and much, much more
- 🚐 Lane Cove Tourist Park

Kiama

Picturesque Kiama is a beautiful coastal town with stunning beaches and delicious fresh produce. Take a stroll through Kiama Terrace shops and visit the local beaches and blowhole.

- ☼ Kiama blowhole, Budderoo National Park, Jamberoo Action Park, Cathedral Rocks, farmers markets, Kiama Terrace shops, Gerringong
- 🚐 BIG4 Easts Beach Holiday Park; Surf Beach Holiday Park
- ⛺ Nungarry Rest Area, Dunmore

Huskisson

Husky is nestled in the Jervis Bay Area, which hosts some of the of the most pristine beaches in Australia, with pure white sand and crystal-clear blue waters. Take a stroll through the township of Huskisson or take a drive out to Green Patch and Hyams Beach.

- ☼ Jervis Bay, whale and dolphin watching
- 🚐 Holiday Haven Huskisson Beach (dog friendly)
- ⛺ Honeymoon Bay Camping (some restrictions); Green Patch Campground
- ☕ Pilgrims

Lake Conjola

An aquatic playground in the Shoalhaven region, ideal for fishing, swimming and boating.

- ☼ Fishing, swimming, visit Bendalong
- 🚐 Holiday Haven Lake Conjola
- ⛺ Milton Showgrounds

Ulladulla

This coastal town and its sandy beaches are beautiful and a must-stop on the South Coast. Plenty of Aboriginal culture to immerse yourself in.

- ☼ Warden Head Lighthouse, Mollymook, Milton, Ulladulla Marina, Cupitt's Winery, Lobster Jack Beach
- 🚐 Ulladulla Headland Holiday Park
- ⛺ Milton Showgrounds
- ☕ Native

Congo Campground

A national park campground situated on an inlet with beautiful beach views. Self-sufficient camping with flushing toilets.

Potato Point

A sweet village with beach views and the remains of an old wharf.

- 🚐 Beachcomber Holiday Park

Narooma

A spectacular part of the NSW South Coast. The amazing blue waters of this area have to be seen to be believed. With some stunning lookouts, Narooma won't disappoint.

☼ Australian Rock, surf beach

🚐 Surf Beach Holiday Park; BIG4 Narooma Easts Holiday Park

⛺ Mystery Bay Campground

Merimbula

The seaside town of Merimbula is a beautiful place to explore. From its waterways and foreshore to some serious fun at Magic Mountain Family Fun Park, there's plenty to do in the area including Ben Boyd National Park and Mimosa Rocks National Park. There are gorgeous beaches and it's only a short daytrip to Eden and Pambula (which also have great caravan parks).

☼ Merimbula Boardwalk, Magic Mountain, Potoroo Palace

🚐 NRMA Merimbula Beach Holiday Park

⛺ The Paddock, Merimbula Bush Camping

AUSTRALIAN CAPITAL TERRITORY

Canberra

The capital city of Australia. Plenty of culture, history and monuments.

☼ Australian War Memorial, Parliament House, National Museum of Australia, Questacon Science & Technology Centre

🚐 Alivio Tourist Park

⛺ Exhibition Park in Canberra; The Truffle Farm

TRIP IN A VAN
—

Tasmania

Boat Harbour
Beach
Devonport
Bay of Fires

Waratah
Launceston

Cradle
Mountain
Bicheno

Strahan
Freycinet
National Park

Derwent Bridge

Salmon Ponds

Hobart

Huonville
Port Arthur

Bruny
Island

Departing Melbourne on the *Spirit of Tasmania*—Big4 Coburg

Big4 Coburg in Melbourne is a fantastic place to start your adventure before heading over Bass Strait on the *Spirit of Tasmania*. It is only twenty-five minutes from the port and the park has great facilities with a pool, heated spa, playgrounds, gym, and great caravan sites and cabins.

There is a Woolworths just down the road, but don't stock up on too much fresh produce as you will lose it all when you go through quarantine at the docks.

Devonport and surrounds

You'll step off the *Spirit of Tasmania* in Devonport, and there is lots to see and do here so allow yourself a few days to explore.

- ☼ Turners Beach Berry Patch, Tasmazia and the Village of Lower Crackpot, Tasmanian Arboretum (find a platypus in the wild!)
- 🚐 Mersey Bluff Caravan Park; Abel Tasman Caravan Park
- ⛺ Horsehead Creek

Penguin and Sulphur Creek

The town of Penguin is only 30km northwest of Devonport. This picturesque seaside town has a gorgeous esplanade and scenic hiking trails. Penguin has a real sense of charm and don't forget to snap a picture with the Big Penguin.

- ☼ Penguin Miniature Railway, a Penguin tour, Penguin Point farming land, Big Penguin statue and playground
- 🚐 Penguin Caravan Park
- ⛺ Preservation Bay to Hall Point, Sulphur Creek

PENGUIN

TURNERS BEACH BERRY PATCH

Boat Harbour Beach

One of the most spectacular beaches in Australia—as you descend into the township you'll be amazed at the colour of the water.

☼ SUP, Rocky Cape National Park, bushwalking, rock pools, wildflowers, walking trails to caves with evidence of Aboriginal settlement, Surfclub House

🚐 Boat Harbour Beach Holiday Park

Stanley and the Nut

Only 50km from Boat Harbour is the gorgeous coastal town of Stanley. It offers uninterrupted views of the long sandy beaches, green hills and preserved colonial buildings. It has also provided a backdrop for a blockbuster movie!

☼ The Nut (take the chairlift or walk the 2km circuit up to the top), Tarkine Wilderness, Highfield Historic Site

🚐 Stanley Cabins & Tourist Park

⛺ Stanley Rec Site (self-contained only)

Waratah—Dip Falls—Cradle Mountain

Take the tourist route towards Dip Falls from Stanley. You can take your caravan in to save you the day trip. To park your caravan when you arrive at Dip Falls, keep going past the Falls towards the 'Big Tree'. There is a track where you can park up your van and then take the short stroll back down to Dip Falls.

Waratah's low-cost camp is a great base if you're exploring Cradle Mountain—it's a forty-five minute drive from the base and information centre. There is a caravan park at Cradle Mountain, but it is a busy one, so we'd recommend booking early if you want a site there.

To get into the Cradle Mountain National Park you'll need a pass which also includes the shuttle bus up to the mountain. There are plenty of walks and hiking trails to do—some take three days and others take twenty minutes. The Dove Lake Walk has two iconic sights along the way—the Boatshed and Glacier Rock—and it's a great walk for the kids.

🚐 Discovery Parks Cradle Mountain, Waratah Caravan Stop

⛺ Conservation Vale of Belvoir

Strahan—Left of Field Campground—Derwent Bridge

Head to the town of Strahan for a look around. A harbourside village that is rich in convict history, it is set in the Tasmanian Wilderness World Heritage Area. As you leave Strahan for Left of Field, it's worth stopping into Derwent Bridge for lunch and to check out The Wall in the Wilderness, an incredible carved sculpture that depicts the history and hardship of those who settled in the area.

- ☼ Left of Field (a serene bush camp with an epic outdoor bath), Russell Falls, West Coast Wilderness Railway steam train tour, Gordon River cruise
- 🚐 Left of Field
- ⛺ Left of Field

Hobart

There's plenty to do in Hobart, a gorgeous waterside city full of history. Park up at Discovery Parks Hobart—it has all the facilities you will need and is only a short drive from the main attractions.

- ☼ Mount Wellington, MONA—Museum of Old and New Art, Salamanca Markets, Richmond, Wicked Cheese Company, Puddleduck Winery
- 🚐 Discovery Parks Hobart
- ⛺ Hobart Showgrounds

Salmon Ponds and Huonville

Drop into the Salmon Ponds for a coffee and a walk around. The kids will love feeding the salmon! Huonville Caravan Park is a very well-run park set on the banks of the river with large grassy sites and plenty of facilities and activities for children. There's a Woolworths in town, so stock up! It's also worth sampling the great coffee at The Local Huonville.

- ☼ Willie Smith Appleshed and Cider, Tahune Air Walk
- 🚐 Huonville Caravan Park
- ⛺ Franklin Camping Ground
- ☕ The Local Huonville

Cockle Creek

About a two-hour drive south of Hobart you hit the access road to Cockle Creek and Southwest National Park. It's 19km of gravel track before you're into the campgrounds. Great fishing here—walk the beach flicking soft plastics and you should catch some flathead for dinner.

The ocean is an amazing blue and the beaches are awesome with beautiful white sand. If you're up for some adventure, the South Cape Track is a four-hour return trek to the southernmost point of Australia.

- ☼ Bronze whale sculpture, 'End of the road' sign, South Cape Walk
- ⛺ Cockle Creek Campground; Boltons Green Campsite
- ⛺ St Albans Bay

THE NECK

PORT ARTHUR HISTORICAL SITE

Bruny Island—Cloudy Bay

Catch the Bruny Island ferry which is about a fifty-minute drive from Hobart. It leaves every half an hour. Camping at Cloudy Bay campground on South Bruny Island is amazing, and you just have to stop into The Neck for a look.

Cloudy Bay campground is accessed via a beach drive. Head along the sand for a few kilometres until you come across the access to the campground.

⛺ Cloudy Bay

Bruny Island—Adventure Bay

The caravan park has a fantastic location and a great atmosphere, and campfires are allowed. Directly opposite the caravan park is the stunning Adventure Bay where you can swim, SUP and try your luck fishing. Keep an eye out for a white wallaby! Check out the several 4WD tracks located around the island. Bruny Island Cruise and Pennicott Wilderness Journeys are excellent ways to explore the rugged coastline.

🚐 Captain Cook Holiday Park

⛺ Neck Game Reserve Camping Area

☕ The Penguin and Paradolte Cafe

Port Arthur

The NRMA Port Arthur Holiday Park is situated five minutes from the Port Arthur Historic Site. It's a lovely park with wildlife including echidnas, pademelons and parrots. It also has a modular pump track for the kids to burn round on their scooters and bikes, a big playground and fire pits at the sites.

☼ Teselated Pavement, Blowhole, Tasman Arch and Devil's Kitchen, Remarkable Cave, Port Arthur Historic Site, Eaglehawk Lookout

🚐 Port Arthur Holiday Park

⛺ Nubeena Ex-Services Club

Freycinet National Park

Freycinet and the surrounding Friendly Beaches are yet more stunning beach landscapes. Freycinet is home to secluded bays, white sandy beaches, mountains and more! A stunning part of Tasmania—you'll need to allow a couple of days to explore properly. There's an IGA, pub and cafe in town.

☀ Wineglass Bay, Mount Amos, Honeymoon Bay, Cape Tourville Lighthouse, Richardson Beach

🚐 BIG4 Iluka on Freycinet Holiday Park

⛺ Freycinet National Park; Friendly Beaches Campground

Bicheno, Douglas Aspley, Swimcart Beach, Bay of Fires

There are so many amazing stretches of coastline on the east coast of Tassie, they are not to be missed! Take your time exploring these incredible landscapes.

☀ Bicheno, Douglas Aspley National Park, Binalong Bay, Sloop Reef, Swimcart Beach, St Helens, Pub in the Paddock, Bay of Fires, Jeanneret Beach and Cosy Corner

🚐 Bicheno East Coast Holiday Park; BIG4 St Helens Holiday Park

⛺ Overnight RV area, Swimcart Beach (has toilets and reception); Cosy Corner; Jeanneret Beach Campground

HONEYMOON BAY

Little Blue Lake and Bridport

The Bridport Seaside Caravan Park is a council-run park on prime real estate with ocean views, an IGA, and good pubs and cafes (especially The Bunker Club) over the road, plus an excellent foreshore walking track and a playground. The park stretches for 2km and there are plenty of private beaches. Don't miss the wonder of the Little Blue Lake.

- ☼ Little Blue Lake Bridport, Pipers Brook Winery, Barnbougle Golf Club, 4WD track to Bellingham
- 🚐 Bridport Seaside Caravan Park
- ⛺ St Albans Bay

Launceston and surrounds

Launceston is a riverside city recognised for the stunning Cataract Gorge, walking trails and gardens. Base yourself at Old Mac's Farm which is a low-cost and self-sufficient campground. Very spacious, it's set on a lake, with large grassy sites and a cafe. Loads of farm animals and paddle boat rides keep the kids entertained, and it's only ten minutes' drive from Launceston City.

- ☼ Launceston City Park, Beauty Point, Seahorse Museum, Platypus World, Beaconsfield Mine (investigate the Tamar Triple Pass), Cataract Gorge, Boags Brewery, Penny Royal, Liffey Falls
- 🚐 BIG4 Launceston Holiday Park
- ⛺ Old Mac's Farm Stay

Bakers Beach Campground

An hour north of Launceston is the Narawntapu National Park, where you'll find Bakers Beach Campground. Facilities include drop toilets, dump point and bins. The great campsites close to the water are awesome for fishing, swimming and hanging out on the sand. Keep an eye out for wombats as well—they cruise around the campground at sunset.

BACK TO THE MAINLAND FROM DEVONPORT

Ask for a late checkout from Mersey Bluff Caravan Park (see page 262) as it's handy not having your van in tow while waiting to sail. For a 7.30pm sail, set off from the park around 5.30pm to get to the *Spirit of Tasmania*, which is only a five-minute drive away.

The night sail is easy and convenient, the cabins have everything you need with bunk beds and an ensuite, and there's great food onboard, plus a playground and movie theatre.

BRIDPORT

CATARACT GORGE

Travel cost calculations

Our budgeting spreadsheet has come about after seven years of travelling Australia and coming to understand exactly what costs are involved when taking your family on the big lap of Oz! Below is an example with our own average travel costs for a family of five to give you an idea of what to expect when you hit the road. The costs will vary for your personal situation, but it's a great starting point!

If you'd like to purchase your own copy of our travel cost calculator, scan the QR code on page 280 and save yourself some budgeting blues.

VARIABLE DESCRIPTION	UNIT	COST	NOTES
ACCOMMODATION COST CALCULATOR			
Average National Park cost per night	AUD	$25	Check the internet for approx prices as they vary from state to state
Average caravan park cost per night	AUD	$70	Price ranges from $28–$100 per night—factor kids in at an extra $5–$15 per night
Free camping cost per night	AUD	$0	The more nights you free camp, the more $$ in your pocket!
Number of nights in National Parks	QTY	8	
Number of nights in caravan parks	QTY	10	
Number of nights free camping	QTY	2	Free camps, roadside stops, friends and family
Approximate monthly accomodation cost		$900	

VARIABLE DESCRIPTION	UNIT	COST	NOTES
FUEL COST CALCULATOR			
Average litres used per 100km	Litre	23	Use a log book or your vehicles dash info to find these figures
Current city price of fuel	AUD	$2.05	At the time of writing, fuel prices have risen dramatically. Be sure to suss out up-to-date trends to calculate your fuel costs.
Remote area fuel loading (20%)	AUD	$0.41	Allow for $0.30 to $0.80 per litre increase in remote towns
Average fuel cost per litre for whole trip	AUD	$2.46	
Estimated total km for trip	KM	40,000	
Number of months travelling	QTY	12	
Approximate monthly fuel cost		$1886	

VARIABLE DESCRIPTION	UNIT	COST	NOTES
FOOD COST CALCULATOR			
Expected average weekly food bill	AUD	$350	Likely to be 10%–20% higher in remote areas. Multiply this weekly cost by 4.3 to get your average monthly cost.
Approximate monthly food cost		$1505.00	

VARIABLE DESCRIPTION	UNIT	COST	NOTES

VEHICLE EXPENDITURE PER MONTH			
Vehicle finance	AUD	$0	Do you have a loan repayment on your vehicle?
Vehicle maintenance	AUD	$250	Servicing, registration, breakdowns, new tyres, windscreen replacement, etc.
Vehicle insurance	AUD	$180	Monthly cost of vehicle insurance
Vehicle registration	AUD	$75	Monthly rego
Approximate monthly vehicle cost		$505	

CARAVAN EXPENDITURE PER MONTH			
Caravan/trailer finance	AUD	$0	Do you have a loan repayment on your caravan/camper trailer?
Caravan/trailer maintenance	AUD	$80	Registration, tyres, repairs, etc.
Caravan/trailer insurance	AUD	$100	Monthly cost of caravan/trailer insurance
Caravan registration	AUD	$30	Monthly rego
Approximate monthly caravan cost		$210	

OTHER EXPENDITURES PER MONTH			
Private health insurance	AUD	$0	If you have private health cover
Attractions/activities	AUD	$250	For example, attractions like zoos and waterparks, etc.
Beer, wine and spirits	AUD	$150	
Dining out/takeaway/coffee	AUD	$60	
Schooling/phone bill	AUD	$280	
Approximate monthly other cost		$740	

UNPLANNED EXPENDITURE PER MONTH			
Extra 5% of net total monthly cost ($5746)	AUD	$287.30	It's always good to have a bit extra just in case!
Approximate monthly unplanned costs		$287.30	

TOTAL MONTHLY TRAVEL EXPENDITURE	AUD	$6033.30

HOME EXPENDITURE PER MONTH			
Mortgage	AUD	$0	Your home mortgage repayments
Home rental expenses	AUD	$0	For example, rates, water, agent fees, maintenance
Home and contents insurance	AUD	$0	Remember to insure your posessions in self storage
Storage of household items	AUD	$100	Self storage shipping container/shed
Mail redirect	AUD	$14.16	This is based on a 12-month Australia Post personal mail redirection package
Credit card repayments	AUD	$0	Your monthly credit card repayments
Other monthly expenses	AUD	$0	For example, schooling, pet sitter, bills
Approximate monthly home cost		$114.16	

TOTAL MONTHLY EXPENDITURE	AUD	$6147.46

INCOME - WHAT MONEY YOU HAVE TO FUND YOUR TRIP			
Starting cash balance (for the whole year)	AUD	$75,000	THIS IS THE TOTAL SAVINGS YOU HAVE FOR THE TRIP. Divide by 12 for your monthly balance.
Additional home income (average/month)	AUD	$0	What you may earn from home, for example rental income, investments, government payments, etc.
Additional travel income (average/month)	AUD	$0	What you expect to earn while travelling, for example seasonal work, online business, etc.
Other	AUD	$0	Anything else, for example work bonus, tax return, early inheritance, etc.
Total income per month		$6250	

Once you have your total monthly income and total monthly expenditure, subtract expenses from income to discover your BALANCE, which is what's left each month. (If this figure isn't in the green then you don't have enough cash for the trip!)

If you have returned a negative figure in your balance, you will need to adjust your expenses or your income until you reach a positive figure. Once that's in the green, you are ready to roll!

NOTE: This is a guide only and not financial advice.

Scan me!

Head to the Trip in a Van website, buy yourself a copy of the original spreadsheet and start planning your trip of a lifetime!

Summary of monthly travel expenditure

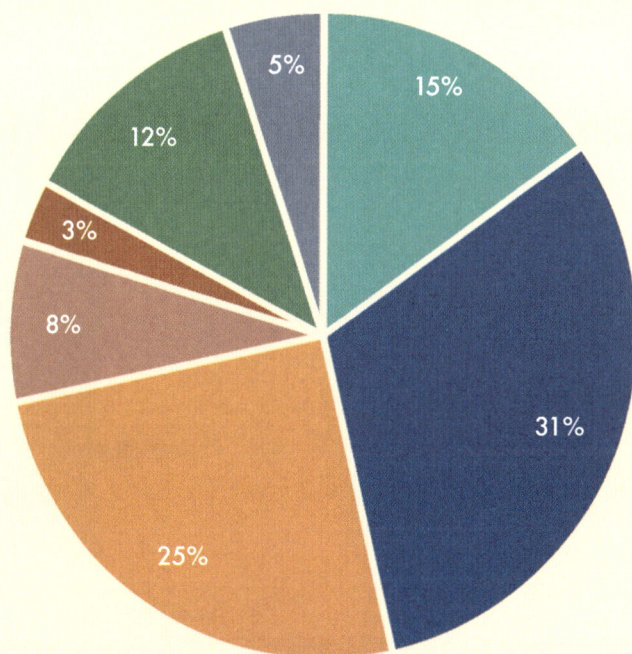

- ● Accomodation costs 15%
- ● Fuel costs 31%
- ● Food costs 25%
- ● Vehicle costs 8%
- ● Caravan costs 3%
- ● Other costs 12%
- ● Unplanned costs 5%

Sample packing list

Caravan

1. Levelling ramps
2. Chocks
3. Trailer coupling lock
4. 40L grey water tank
5. Impact gun
6. Sand pegs
7. Hex pegs
8. Annex flooring
9. Shade screen Protector (back/front and side)
10. Water filter
11. Power lead 25m and an extra
12. Water hose 2 x 10m and an extra
13. Hose and lead bags
14. Various hose fittings
15. Handheld vacuum
16. Water storage tanks
17. Water filtration and cartridges
18. Floor mat
19. Dustpan and brush
20. Trailer hitch lock
21. Broom
22. Diesel heater
23. 12v LED lights
24. Generator and inverter
25. 240v power board
26. Amphibian power adaptor
27. Spare caravan and car keys
28. Small bin for inside
29. Large bin for outside

Furniture

1. Folding clothesline
2. Folding table
3. Deck chairs
4. Kids' deck chairs
5. Kids' foldable picnic table
6. Outdoor pantry
7. Washing machine

Gadgets

1. iPad
2. iPad charger
3. iPad cover
4. DVD player
5. GoPro
6. iPod
7. Phone
8. Phone charger
9. Walkie talkie
10. Laptop
11. Laptop charger
12. External hard drive
13. Dash camera
14. TV and antenna
15. Camera—kids
16. DLSR camera
17. Drone
18. Binoculars
19. Wifi unit
20. Bluetooth speaker
21. Hairdryer
22. 12v fans
23. Tripod

Kitchen

1. Electric frypan
2. Frypan
3. 1 x large saucepan
4. 1x medium saucepan
5. 1x small saucepan
6. Colander
7. Mixing bowls
8. Toaster
9. Thermos
10. Cake and muffin tin
11. Cooling rack
12. 2 x chopping boards
13. 1 large mixing and salad bowl (collapsible)
14. Strainer
15. Dish drying rack
16. Bottle opener
17. Can opener
18. Corkscrew
19. Mixing spoon
20. Various plastic containers
21. Toaster
22. Jaffle maker
23. 1x serving platter
24. Tongs
25. Spatula
26. Grater
27. Potato masher
28. BBQ
29. Knives
30. Forks
31. Tablespoons
32. Teaspoons
33. Kids' cutlery
34. Plates
35. Wine tumbler

36. Drinking cups/glasses
37. Drink bottles
38. Kids' plastic cups
39. Travel mugs
40. Billy
41. Kettle
42. Pots and pans
43. Tea towels
44. Broom
45. Fly swatter
46. Coffee machine and milk frother
47. Dinner set
48. Blender
49. Portable gas stove
50. Cooking plate/grill
51. Thermomix
52. Kitchen knife
53. Knife sharpener
54. Bread knife
55. Stubby cooler(s)
56. Vegie peeler
57. Dishwashing tub
58. Dishwashing detergent
59. Dish cloth and scourer
60. Absorbent dish drying mat
61. Paper towel
62. Rubbish bags/bin liners
63. Sandwich press
64. Sandwich bags
65. Baking paper
66. Cling wrap
67. Aluminium foil
68. Entertaining plate for nibbles
69. Toothpicks
70. BBQ tools
71. Sanitiser
72. Fire extinguisher
73. Fire blanket
74. Tissues
75. Baby wipes
76. Highchair
77. Bumbo
78. Bibs
79. Small inside kitchen bin

Food

1. Cereal
2. Quick oats
3. Baked beans/spaghetti
4. Bread
5. Vegemite
6. Jam
7. Honey
8. Peanut butter
9. Maple syrup
10. Pancake mix
11. Fruit
12. Muesli bars
13. Cruskits/dry biscuits
14. Cheese
15. Ham/chicken
16. Tomato sauce
17. BBQ sauce
18. Salt
19. Pepper
20. Stock
21. Cooking oil/spray
22. Spices
23. Eggs
24. Bacon
25. Sausages
26. Roast meat
27. Tuna
28. Fresh vegetables
29. Frozen vegetables
30. Rice
31. Pasta
32. Noodles
33. Coconut cream
34. Milk
35. Long-life milk
36. Flour
37. Self-raising flour
38. Happy hour snacks
39. Butter
40. Crackers
41. Chips
42. Dips
43. Bread crumbs
44. Seasoning mix
45. Marshmallows
46. Beer
47. Wine
48. Spirits
49. Drinking water
50. Tea
51. Coffee
52. Drinking chocolate

Off the grid

1. Billy kettle
2. Portable solar panels
3. Air mattress
4. Tent
5. Sleeping bags
6. 12V shower
7. Portable toilet
8. Water jerry cans x 2
9. Butane gas cooker and cartridges
10. 12V LED strip lights
11. Shower/toilet tent
12. Swags
13. Camp stretcher
14. Hammock
15. Camp bunks
16. Mosquito nets
17. Jaffle iron
18. Camp oven

Communications and apps

1. Camps8
2. Wiki Camps App
3. Fuel Maps App
4. Track My Tour App
5. UHF handheld radios
6. UHF radio
7. Satellite phone
8. GPS
9. Hema Navigation
10. EPIRB
11. Foldable maps

Clothes

1. Beach towels for each
2. Bath towel x 3
3. Face washer

Kids (per child)

1. 4 x shorts
2. 4 x t-shirts
3. 2 x dresses
4. 2 x jumpers
5. 2 x trousers
6. 2 x summer pyjamas
7. 2 x winter pyjamas
8. 6 x underwear
9. 2 x socks
10. 2 x swimmers
11. 1 x rashie
12. 1 x hat
13. 1 x thongs
14. 1 x runners
15. 1 x slip on/Converse/ dress shoes
16. 1 x winter/rain jacket

Women

1. 4 x shorts
2. 4 x t-shirts
3. 4 x singlets
4. 2 x dresses
5. 1 x jeans
6. 2 x long sleeve top
7. 2 x jumpers
8. 2 x track pants
9. 1 x dressy top
10. 1 x leggings
11. 2 x workout leggings
12. 2 x workout singlet
13. 1 x set of pyjamas
14. 2 x swimmers
15. 1 x cap
16. 1 x full brim hat
17. 1 x sunglasses
18. 1 x reading glasses
19. 1 x thongs
20. 1 x sandals
21. 1 x runners
22. 1 x flats/Converse
23. 3 x socks
24. 6 x underwear
25. 3 x t-shirt bras
26. 2 x sport bras
27. 1 x winter/rain jacket
28. 1 x beanie

Men

1. 4 x shorts
2. 4 x t-shirts
3. 4 x singlets
4. 1 x jeans
5. 1 x jumper
6. 1 x track pants
7. 2 x workout shorts
8. 2 x workout singlets
9. 2 x swimmer shorts
10. 1 x set of pyjamas
11. 1 x cap
12. 1 x sunglasses
13. 1 x beanie
14. 1 x thongs
15. 1 x winter/rain jacket
16. 1 x runners
17. 3 x socks
18. 6 x underwear

Toiletries

1. Shampoo
2. Conditioner
3. Sanitary products
4. Toothbrush and toothpaste
5. Hairbrush
6. Contraception
7. Dry shampoo
8. Deodorant
9. Soap
10. Face wash
11. Shaver
12. Shaving cream
13. Day moisturiser
14. Night/eye cream
15. Makeup
16. Prescription medication
17. Sunscreen
18. Hand sanitiser
19. Toiletry bag
20. Face washer
21. Hairspray
22. Hair gel
23. Hair ties and accessories

Car

1. Portable fridge
2. MaxTraxx
3. 12V air compressor
4. Tyre deflators
5. Shovel
6. GPS
7. UHF radio
8. Fishing rod holders
9. Reversing camera
10. Tyre repair kit—plugs, patches, valves
11. Fire extinguisher
12. Fuel jerry can
13. First aid and snake bite kit
14. Car seat organisers

Miscellaneous

1. Kids' scooters
2. Kids' bikes and helmets
3. Adult bike
4. Pram
5. Highchair/Bumbo
6. Spare blankets
7. Minimal toys
8. Lego and activity books
9. Box of craft supplies
10. Deck of cards and board games
11. Sporting equipment
12. Beach toys and bucket and spade
13. DVDs/Movies/USBs
14. Torches/headlamps
15. Backpacks
16. Child carrier
17. Various fishing rods
18. Reels and tackle
19. Pool noodles
20. Snorkelling gear
21. Toilet paper
22. Toilet chemical
23. Drink bottles
24. Occy straps
25. Washing basket (foldable)
26. Laundry powder
27. Batteries
28. Boogie boards
29. Canoe/kayak
30. Stand-up paddleboard
31. Surfboard
32. Boardgames
33. Cards
34. Basketball/football
35. Cricket bat and ball
36. Frisbee
37. Collapsible pantry/ wardrobe
38. Beach umbrella
39. Sunscreen
40. Floatie/swim vest
41. Hiking backpack
42. Hiking poles
43. Mosquito coils
44. Insect repellent

First aid kit

1. Panadol
2. Ibuprofen
3. Bandaids
4. Asprin
5. Gastro-Stop
6. Laxatives
7. Throat lozenges
8. Saline solution
9. Aquaear ear drops
10. Ear plugs
11. First aid guide
12. Vomit bag
13. Wipes
14. Tweezers
15. Scissors
16. Soov
17. Eucalyptus oil
18. Calamine lotion
19. Cotton balls/pads
20. Ear buds
21. Cough mixture
22. Asthma puffer
23. Opsite
24. Crepe bandages
25. Triangle bandages
26. Latex gloves
27. Betadine cream

Accessories

1. Tent pegs
2. Sand pegs
3. Ratchet straps
4. Pocket knife
5. Shovel
6. Tarp
7. Mallet

Tool box & spare parts

1. Volt impact wrench for wheel nuts
2. Volt battery charger for vehicle
3. Jumper cables—heavy duty
4. Spanner set—open ended
5. Shifting spanner—small
6. Shifting spanner—medium
7. Shifting spanner—large
8. Socket set
9. Allen keys
10. Vice grips
11. Pliers—long nose
12. Spare car key
13. Screwdrivers—Phillips head
14. Screwdrivers—flat
15. Wheel brace
16. Bottle or scissor jack
17. Small hydraulic jack and handle
18. Cordless drill
19. Drill bits
20. Multimeter
21. Soldering iron 12V and solder
22. Duct tape
23. Electrical/insulation tape—roll
24. Electrical wire—roll
25. Electrical connectors—assorted
26. Electrical crimping tool
27. WD-40
28. Degreaser
29. Workshop manual
30. Hand cleaner
31. Rags
32. Disposable gloves
33. Oil filter removal tool
34. Small axe
35. Battery chainsaw
36. Cable ties, assorted
37. Grease gun with grease
38. Funnel
39. Small tarp
40. Jack stands
41. Silicon spray
42. Bar's Leaks Stop Leak
43. Metal bond—Knead It
44. Vehicle tools
45. Butane torch
46. Brush set—steel, copper, plastic
47. Old toothbrush
48. Ice cream container
49. Magnetic tray
50. Bucket or tub for draining oil
51. Light or torch
52. Oil, fuel and air filters
53. Wheel bearing kit—trailer/caravan
54. Grease—wheel bearing
55. Fan belts—complete set
56. Assorted nuts, bolts, screws
57. Hose clamps—various sizes
58. Globes for indicators, brakes, etc
59. Silastic or similar sealant
60. Gasket silicon or liquid gasket
61. Tape
62. Silicone
63. Fuses
64. Rope

Recovery gear

1. Long handled shovel
2. Maxtrax or GTreds
3. Snatch strap
4. Snatch block
5. Tree protector straps
6. Winch on vehicle
7. Winch extension straps
8. Rated bow shackles
9. Leather rigger gloves
10. Storage bag for recovery gear
11. Ground sheet
12. Drawbar recovery hitch with D shackle

Bedding

1. Doona/comforter
2. Doona cover
3. Pillow
4. Pillow case
5. Flat sheet
6. Fitted sheet
7. Teddies and dolls
8. Euro pillows
9. Spare blankets for cool nights

Your own extras

1.
2.
3.
4.
5.
6.
7.
8.
9.
10.
11.
12.
13.
14.
15.
16.
17.
18.
19.
20.

Index

Good luck!

Keep in touch with us on our socials

⊙ @tripinavan   ▶ Trip in a Van

tripinavan.com.au

ALLEN&UNWIN
SYDNEY · MELBOURNE · AUCKLAND · LONDON

We have in no way been affiliated with these caravan parks, campsites or attractions and activities. These are from our own personal experience and 100% OUR advice only.

If you come across a campsite or caravan park that has been disappointing, has since closed down or has changed in some way from our review, we would love to know. We'd like to continue improving and updating this itinerary. Please email us at tripinavan@gmail.com.

First published in 2022

Copyright © Rebecca and Justin Lorrimer 2022

All rights reserved. No part of this book may be reproduced or transmitted in any form or by any means, electronic or mechanical, including photocopying, recording or by any information storage and retrieval system, without prior permission in writing from the publisher. *The Australian Copyright Act 1968* (the Act) allows a maximum of one chapter or 10 per cent of this book, whichever is the greater, to be photocopied by any educational institution for its educational purposes provided that the educational institution (or body that administers it) has given a remuneration notice to the Copyright Agency (Australia) under the Act.

Allen & Unwin
83 Alexander Street
Crows Nest NSW 2065
Australia
Phone: (61 2) 8425 0100
Email: info@allenandunwin.com
Web: www.allenandunwin.com

A catalogue record for this book is available from the National Library of Australia

ISBN 978 1 76106 752 5

Internal design and maps by Kirby Armstrong
Cover design by Kirby Armstrong
All images by Bec and Justin Lorrimer
Index by Kerryn Burgess
Printed by C & C Offset Printing Co., Ltd, China

10 9 8 7 6 5 4 3

MIX
Paper | Supporting responsible forestry
FSC® C008047